TEEN PREGNANCY

A Special Report from the
Education Research Group
Roberta Weiner, Executive Editor

Ministry of Education, Ontario
Information Centre, 16th Floor
Mowat Block, Queen's Park
Toronto, Ont.

Capitol Publications, Inc.,
1101 King Street, Alexandria, Virginia 22314

Also published by the Education Research Group:

The Child Abuse Crisis: Impact on the Schools
P.L. 94-142: Impact on the Schools
AIDS: Impact on the Schools
Education Directory: A Guide to Decisionmakers in the Federal Government, the States and Education Associations
Inside the Education Department: An Office-by-Office Review
Education Regulations Library
The Education Evaluator's Workbook: How to Assess Education Programs
The Supreme Court and Education
Education Sourcebook: Where to Find the Materials You Need
The 1986 Tax Reform Act: Bad News for Nonprofits
Proven Plans for Recruiting and Retaining Students: 21 Case Studies

Copyright © 1987 by the Education Research Group, Capitol Publications, Inc.,

Helen Hoart, Publisher
Roberta Weiner, Executive Editor

All rights reserved. No part of this book may be reproduced or used in any form without permission in writing from the publisher. Address inquiries to: Education Research Group, Capitol Publications, Inc., 1101 King St., Alexandria, Va. 22314.

Printed in the United States of America

Library of Congress Catalog Card Number 86-83248
ISBN 0-937925-03-9

Weiner, Roberta
Teen Pregnancy: Impact on the Schools

Cover design by Linda C. McDonald and Sue Gubisch

First Edition

Table of Contents

Introduction..Page 5

Chapter One
Pregnant Teens Move Into The Mainstream......................Page 7

Chapter Two
A Question Of Responsibility: The School's Role In
Pregnancy Prevention..Page 17

Chapter Three
After The Fact: Helping Pregnant And Parenting Teens...........Page 37

Case Studies

Case Study #1
Sexuality Education And Counseling Program, Teen Choice,
New York City Public Schools..Page 47

Case Study #2
Mini Schools For Pregnant Teens, Pregnant Adolescent
Continuing Education, Minneapolis School District.............Page 53

Case Study #3
Adolescent Parenting Program, Cambridge Rindge And
Latin School, Cambridge, Mass.......................................Page 57

Case Study #4
Junior High Decisionmaking Curriculum, San Marcos, Calif.,
Junior High School...Page 61

Case Study #5
Teen Theater Troupe, New Orleans Center For Creative
Arts And Planned Parenthood Of Louisiana.......................Page 69

Appendices

Appendix A
Survey Results..Page 79

Appendix B
Bibliography...Page 89

Appendix C
From Our Rolodex..Page 93

Introduction

U.S. teens under age 15 are at least 15 times more likely to give birth than their peers in any other Western nation. More than 1 million teenage girls in the United States become pregnant every year. Some 400,000 teenagers have abortions each year and 470,000 others—the majority of whom are unmarried—give birth.

While some try to quiet fears by pointing out that the figures haven't increased since the 1970s, teen pregnancy continues to be a thorny issue for school administrators.

Further complicating the matter is a doubt over whether sex education programs can really prevent pregnancy. And supporters of those programs are trying their best to let educators know that classes are only part of the answer.

Asta-Maria Kenney, associate for policy development at the Alan Guttmacher Institute in Washington, D.C., believes "the mission of schools is education, and kids have a crying need" for sex education information. But she also points out that those courses have limitations: less than half of sex education courses even have prevention as a goal. Fewer, of course, meet that goal.

A critical component of pregnancy prevention is access to birth control, a point of view that got a hefty boost in December 1986 when the National Research Council urged schools to include information in sex education classes on how to obtain and use contraceptives. Yet contraception is an aspect of sex education that most schools neglect or deliberately ignore. In a survey the Education Research Group conducted for this report, 96 percent of school administrators responding said their districts do not provide birth control to students (see Appendix A for full survey results).

Anecdotal proof that schools are failing to adequately educate students is prevalent. David Bass offers this story. As coordinator of Concerned Black Men, a Washington, D.C., organization that believes men need to be more involved in issues such as teen pregnancy, he frequently speaks to students. He asks them to name three sexually transmitted diseases. One time, a boy in the audience thought and thought and finally told him, "Poison ivy." "If you leave it for them to get [the information] in the streets, they'll get it wrong," Bass said.

* * *

6   Teen Pregnancy: Impact on the Schools

This special report from the Education Research Group is designed to help school administrators set up or revise teen pregnancy and parenting programs in their schools. Chapter One analyzes the results of our survey of some 700 school administrators on their attitudes toward the teen pregnancy problem. Chapters Two and Three discuss what schools are now doing for pregnant and parenting teens.

The five case studies offer a potpourri of success stories. Administrators can borrow entire programs or can choose certain elements that may work in their district. At the beginning of each case study are contacts administrators can get in touch with to learn more details about the programs.

* * *

The major contributors to this report were James Buie and David Lytle. Jim, a staff writer with the Education Research Group (ERG), researched and wrote Chapter 1 with the assistance of Jeffrey Fanger, an ERG student intern from George Washington University. Dave, editor of the Capitol Publications newsletter *Nation's Schools Report*, did much of the research and writing for Chapters 2 and 3. Also contributing to the research was Sean Hadden, an ERG student intern from Colorado State University.

The five case studies were written by education reporters and freelance writers and researchers who live in or near the cities housing the programs; each researcher visited the program at least once. They are credited following the individual case studies.

Thanks also go to ERG's managing editor, Leslie A. Ratzlaff, for assisting in the copyediting and production of the report; editorial assistant Christopher Grasso, for many hours of proofreading and fact-checking; Rosette Graham, our production manager; Cynthia Peters, our typesetter; Linda McDonald, our graphic artist; and our marketing and circulation staff: Kristan S. Winters, Tammy Vagias, Allison Sator, Ellen Carroll, Barbara L. Davis, Gloria Smith, Joan Rodriguez and Robin Carey. My appreciation to Helen Hoart for her thoughtful critiques of the manuscript. And to Jackie Manley and Lana Muraskin, thanks for taking the time to share your experiences and encourage us to proceed with the project.

Roberta Weiner
Executive Editor
Education Research Group

Chapter One

Pregnant Teens Move Into The Mainstream

In 1986, nearly 45 percent of students ages 11 to 18 in the Fresno, Calif., schools were estimated to be sexually active. In the preceding three years, 15 percent of the female students 11 to 18 had become pregnant.

Yet in Fresno, few citizens expressed a desire to isolate pregnant teens and teen parents, to send them to special schools or to punish them for their "wayward" behavior. The Fresno school system not only mainstreamed pregnant teens and teen parents; it provided full-time child care and classes in parenting and child nutrition.

Fresno's program of mainstreaming pregnant teens and teen parents and providing services for them is more comprehensive than most. Yet the trend toward mainstreaming has garnered widespread support across the nation. A survey the Education Research Group (ERG) conducted exclusively for *Teen Pregnancy: Impact on the Schools* found that the vast majority of school officials — 80 percent — support mainstreaming pregnant teens and teen parents.

Lana Muraskin, a former teen pregnancy researcher with the National Association of State Boards of Education (NASBE), found the results of the ERG study "very encouraging." A few years ago, she said, "you would have found a great deal of hostility to visibly pregnant adolescents." The trend toward mainstreaming, she said, is "very healthy." Alternative facilities for pregnant teens and teen parents may be warm and supportive environments, said Muraskin, but they are generally inferior educationally.

The ERG survey demonstrated just how dramatically attitudes have changed since the Victorian era when girls who became pregnant out of wedlock were shamed or shunted off to live with relatives because their families were too scandalized to face the community.

Even in rural school districts, where attitudes might be expected to be less "sophisticated," officials embraced mainstreaming as a practical necessity, according to the ERG study. "You can't very well shave off their heads and put crosses on their foreheads," said Richard Wolford, superintendent of the tiny (850-student) Greenwood, S.D., school system.

Wolford said teen pregnancy is among the top five problems his district faces. Yet the problem seems to fluctuate from year to year. "Some years it's the trendy thing to do, like engagements were" a generation ago. In more innocent, less complicated times, a rural school district could expect a flurry of engagements in a given year, if the idea caught on. In the 1980s, Wolford said, students are more likely to skip the formalities of marriage and just have babies. Wolford saw no disadvantages to mainstreaming. In fact, including teen parents in school may help to show kids that "there's no excitement in being a teen parent."

Janice Klemm, director of the School-Age Parenting Program in Fresno and coordinator of the Consumer Home Economics and Family Life Education program, agrees. School-based programs expose students to the full responsibilities of parenthood, she said. They "take the romanticism out of having a baby."

Klemm and Wolford were among 716 school officials from across the nation who responded to an ERG survey on teen pregnancy and parenting. Nearly 80 percent of the respondents, or precisely 79.2 percent, were from rural school districts, 15 percent were from suburban school districts, and 4.6 percent were from urban school districts. While the survey was not scientifically designed to ensure demographic representation (ERG sent surveys to a random selection of the nation's 15,445 school superintendents, but in the returned surveys, rural school districts were over-represented), educators nevertheless vouched for its significance.

"You can't very well shave off their heads and put crosses on their foreheads."
—Richard Wolford, superintendent, Greenwood, S.D., school system

Among the more significant results (for a complete breakdown of results, see Appendix A):

■ 62 percent of the respondents said mainstreaming has no effect on other teens, while 25.3 percent said mainstreaming discourages teens from getting pregnant.

■ Some 66 percent believed the sex education available in their school district reduces teen pregnancy, though they acknowledged "it's just a hunch." Just 5.9 percent said they had substantial evidence to support the belief that sex education reduces teen pregnancy, while 26.2 percent said sex education does not reduce teen pregnancy.

These results demonstrate, Muraskin said, that "people in the field are becoming increasingly aware of the research," research that consistently has shown that sex education programs have little impact on teen pregnancy rates. For years, educators, particularly teachers, liked to think they could substantially reduce sexual activity and teen pregnancy by instituting "the right program." They have finally come to realize that "sex education is not a powerful treatment for teen pregnancy," said Muraskin, who is now with the U.S. Education Department.

More basic factors, such as an adolescent's self-esteem, personal goals, support system, value system, home environment and family income level help shape sexual decisions, Muraskin said.

■ School administrators seemed divided on the question of whether birth control should be provided to students as part of comprehensive health clinic services. Nearly 40 percent said no, 30 percent said yes (with parent's permission), and 27 percent said yes without a provision for parental permission. At the same time, 96 percent of the school officials said their districts did not provide birth control to students.

These percentages revealed broad-based support from school administrators for the idea of providing birth control to students, Muraskin noted. A clear majority of 57 percent approved, when combining the 27 percent who said birth control should be provided to students as part of health clinic services with the 30 percent who said yes with parental permission. Such support was surprising, Muraskin said. "School administrators are supposed to be more cautious" than the public in general.

> *School-based programs "take the romanticism out of having a baby."*
> —Janice Klemm, director, School Age Parenting Program, Fresno, Calif.

Such results, she said, are "very encouraging," and may help to establish more pregnancy prevention programs in schools.

On the other hand, while administrators may favor the concept of providing birth control to students, it's doubtful they would take the lead in instituting on-campus programs that provide birth control to students, said Scott Thomson, executive director of the National Association of Secondary School Principals. "School officials are divided because the public is divided," he said. "Schools pretty much reflect society at large."

"I have a hunch," Thomson said, "that the vast majority [of the public] would be opposed to providing birth control on high school campuses." It's unlikely, he added, that school officials would be willing to institute a program that might incite community opposition.

Mainstreaming in most cases seems to be best for pregnant teens, Thomson said, as long as the teens are offered—at a minimum—courses in prenatal care and child development. As long as such special instruction is available, he added, mainstreaming has many more positive than negative aspects.

Thomson agreed with administrators who said sex education had little impact on teen pregnancy rates. California schools have required sex education for more than 30 years, he said, yet California also has one of the highest rates of sexual activity and teen pregnancy in the nation.

"The survey results are quite interesting," said Gary Marx, associate executive director of the American Association of School Administrators (AASA). "We had sensed a growing concern among school administrators about teen pregnancy, and this study confirms it."

If, as the survey suggests, nearly 65 percent of school administrators viewed teen pregnancy as one of the top 10 problems their school system faces (21.6 percent said it's among the top five problems), perhaps a major national initiative would be appropriate, Marx said.

> *School officials finally have come to realize that "sex education is not a powerful treatment for teen pregnancy."*
> — Lana Muraskin, teen pregnancy researcher, Washington, D.C.

While school administrators in the ERG study did not express much confidence in the ability of sex education courses to stem the tide of teen pregnancy, they still agreed that schools have a large responsibility to deal with issues of teen sexuality. And they gave the strong impression that schools traditionally do too little, too late, about teen sexuality.

One administrator, Ann Rogers, project manager for TAPP (Teenage Alternative Pregnancy Program), a Monmouth County Educational Services Commission alternative school program in Eatontown, N.J., was in the minority on the issue of mainstreaming. She said mainstreaming, for the most part, "does not help pregnant teens and teen parents significantly address their unique problems."

Mainstreaming, she said, can be cruel. Many of the students in her program actually prefer to be separated from the mainstream. "When you're eight months pregnant, and you can't fit into your desk, and everybody laughs at you, it takes a tough little kid to survive."

TAPP mixes academic courses with a unique combination of pre- and postnatal instruction, home economics, consumer education, money and time management, and employability skills. The program offers individual and group counseling and classes designed to prepare students for child care, childbirth, child development and parenting.

From its inception in 1981 through 1986, TAPP served 245 girls ages 12 to 19. The program, which was budgeted at $92,800 in 1985, operates on a separate campus from the regular high school, and instruction is geared to individual needs and learning styles.

As evidence of the value of early intervention programs with pregnant teens, Rogers noted that babies born to girls in the program have weighed a healthy average of six pounds, five ounces at birth, more than the national average. Additionally, 89 percent of the pregnant teens in the program have returned to school to complete their educations.

Rogers justified the program as an investment in the future. "If these young people are going to break the cycle, they're going to need support services and a little something extra." Programs like TAPP are less controversial for most communities than school-based clinics, especially if school-based clinics try to provide birth control.

New York and Chicago both have been embroiled in controversies over the provision of birth control to high school students, with vehement opposition from certain members of the communities. Rogers would just as soon avoid those controversies in her community, she said, though she could understand why some school systems resort to such drastic measures. In certain areas of New York and Chicago, where teen pregnancy has reached epidemic proportions, "if I were them, I'd put birth control in the drinking water," Rogers said.

Public Opinion Surveys

Correlating the ERG study with 1985 Gallup and Harris polls suggests that school administrators and the public need to communicate better about what they want and what they believe can be appropriately done in public schools.

In separate surveys, both school administrators and the public seemed to think the schools should do more about the problems of teen pregnancy and teen parenting, but they both seemed hesitant to broach the subject.

Administrators seemed to fear the public would accuse them of going too far, and they were not sure they would have the political and financial support of the public or legislators. The public, on the other hand, expressed strong support for sex education in general, but seemed to wonder what it would entail specifically.

A 1985 Louis Harris poll showed 85 percent of the public supported sex education in the schools. And a Gallup poll the same year found that 85 percent of those supporting sex education favored instruction on birth control in high school and 48 percent favored instruction in elementary school.

Although the data are less complete, there was evidence of support for sex education programs among school administrators as well. A 1982 survey by Planned Parenthood found that 82 percent of school board members and superintendents in Bible-belt Indiana approved of sex education, with 49 percent stating that contraception was an essential topic. Another 31 percent thought the topic should "probably" be included.

California Programs

California has been aware of the problem perhaps longer than any other state. It began to develop comprehensive programs for pregnant teens and teen parents as early as 1974. By 1986, school-age parenting centers were set up on six high school campuses in Fresno, with a total budget of $100,000. Statewide, the 1986 budget for the program was $6.7 million.

Fresno program director Janice Klemm described the services provided: a full day's child care, from 7:30 a.m. to 4 p.m., for all teen parents; three registered nurses on hand to care for the children, keep their health records and offer mothers parenting tips; diapers, formula and food for the babies while their mothers are in class; child development activities; and classes in parenting skills. Fresno's seven on-campus centers in 1985-86 served 300 teenagers and their babies.

When adolescents seek pregnancy counseling, Klemm said the program nurses are required to offer referrals to three different types of clinics — one that approves of abortion, one that opposes abortion and a third that takes a middle-of-the-road approach.

When the program first started, a few members of the Fresno community snidely referred to it as "the baby factory," and suggested pregnant teens and teen parents should receive no special attention or special services. "They made their beds. Now they should lie in them," was a frequently expressed attitude, Klemm said. Most of the complaints died down after a few years, Klemm added, as people began to realize how cost-effective the program was.

"The long-range cost to the taxpayers for welfare and aid to families with dependent children is much more than this," she said.

For example, if a teenager has her first child at age 15, it will cost taxpayers $18,130 over the following 20 years, according to the National Research Council. If the schools can intervene early enough in a child's life to see that basic needs are met, the child's chances of living a normal, productive life are enhanced, Klemm said.

Sensitivity To The Community

Administrators emphasized that they have to be sensitive to the values of people in their communities. Carl Shaff, superintendent of the Rogue River, Ore., School District #35, a district of 1,200 students with a high incidence of teen pregnancy, said home and church still form the foundation for a student's values. "A strong home life is the foundation to proper attitudes about sex," he said. "Many people in my community believe we [school officials] should keep our noses out of it."

"We have to be real careful," Shaff said. Sex education, if it is handled properly, with trained professionals, can be helpful, but there are definite limits to what the schools can do. Providing detailed birth control information or dispensing birth control would not be a good idea. "I've got lots of other problems without opening that can of worms," he said.

Wolford emphasized that in his rural school district, parental autonomy has to be respected. "Sex education is, to a large extent, viewed as a parental prerogative," he said. The schools face numerous restrictions on what they can teach and how far they can go. "If we brought in Planned Parenthood, I don't think we'd have a sex education program."

In his district, Wolford said, schools would be hard pressed to refer students to the local health clinic without parental permission. On occasions when that has happened, the parents "raised the devil because they weren't aware of it," he said.

In many communities, bad economic conditions create an atmosphere that breeds teenage parents. Las Vegas, N.M., a town of about 12,500 in the northern part of the state, has an unemployment rate of nearly 18 percent, said Christino Griego, a counselor in the Las Vegas city schools. "We have minimal employment opportunity, and that has caused family breakups, single parenting and a lack of supervision," he said.

Griego said the Las Vegas school system fails to give students enough information about sex. "Kids are still basically ignorant." While students are required to take a health class that deals with the consequences of drug abuse and teenage sex, it is not intensive enough, nor does it provide practical information about birth control, he said.

Part of the reluctance of the school system to deal directly with the issue, Griego said, is the strong religious taboo against open discussion of sexual conduct. Las Vegas is 80 percent Catholic, and very traditional when it comes to male and female roles, he said. "For a girl to look her dad in the eye and tell him she needs birth control is still a disgrace," he said. Boys, on the other hand, are winked at by their fathers if they "score" with a girl.

"Maybe the way to get teenagers to be more responsible is through the males," Griego said. "If we could somehow play on the notion that it's macho to carry around prophylactics, well, let's encourage them to use them."

In many small communities such as Las Vegas, Griego said, there is also fear of exposure and not enough privacy. Students can't go down to the health clinic to discuss sexual problems or the need for contraception without running into a cousin, the best friend of a parent, or some other person they know. People in small communities have reputations to uphold, and they shy away from the facilities that could offer help, Griego said.

> "School officials are divided because the public is divided. Schools pretty much reflect society at large."
> —Scott Thomson, executive director, National Association of Secondary School Principals

While strong religious values may still inhibit some students from irresponsible sexual behavior, these same values, if narrowly enforced on a community, can actually prevent people from dealing with reality. Griego noted that in a neighboring school district, a large contingent of fundamentalists rallied in opposition to drug education in schools. They argued that such issues are not proper areas of discussion topics for schools. These people feel the same way about sex education, and create such a tense, adversarial atmosphere that more "enlightened" people are afraid to speak out. "People don't want to be condemned to hell," Griego said.

Home environment, most administrators said, is still the most important ingredient in determining the attitudes and behavior of students. "The schools can only do so much," said Louis Digirolamo, superintendent of the small Scio, N.Y., school system, with 620 pupils.

"I know a woman who's between her third and fourth husband, and double-dating with her daughter," Digirolamo said. "When one

Pregnant Teens Move Into The Mainstream 15

of her daughters got pregnant, the mother's only worry seemed to be whether her daughter would be too fat for the prom."

With the high divorce rate and so many single-parent families, children grow up with distorted ideas about what family life should be like, Digirolamo said. He related an incident in one fifth-grade class where the students were discussing single parent families. One little girl whose parents had divorced popped up to say she was not a member of a single parent family. "I'm lucky," she said. "My mommy sleeps with a different daddy every night."

Nevertheless, Digirolamo and numerous other school officials expressed the belief that sexual irresponsibility among teenagers is declining for many reasons, including fear of AIDS and other sexually transmitted diseases, a resurgence of religious values, and the increasing effectiveness of institutions such as schools to deal with the problem.

"We're seeing less of the wild teenage parties," Digirolamo said. "The kids are definitely backing off."

Strategies With The Community

The ERG study also found that many school officials who believed their systems were effectively dealing with teen pregnancy had consciously cultivated the support of their communities, allowing parents to express their views as programs developed.

In suburban Selma, Calif., for example, Superintendent Steve Bojorguez noted that a drive for teenage sex education had begun in the community, not the schools. A group of parents started a sex education program for adolescents, and established enough credibility to garner school support.

"We have had lots of community involvement from the start," said Thomas E. Neel, superintendent of the Show Low, Ariz., school district. In designing a school policy on teen pregnancy, Neel said, his system first surveyed students, then published the results of the survey in the local newspaper. Publicizing the results of the survey dramatized the issue and focused local public opinion in favor of a program for pregnant teens, Neel said.

Opening up the sex education curriculum for community discussion helped establish a consensus on what should be taught, said Cathy Tibbett, superintendent of the Fremont, Iowa, school system. The mental health and medical communities offered helpful suggestions, and so did many of the parents. But Tibbett acknowledged that opening up the sex education curriculum for community discussion involved risks. "As an administrator, you've got to be willing to take the heat for a little while until the program is started."

Some administrators felt a strategy of openness was not worth the risks. Public discussion of sex education, they said, was too inflammatory, with too much potential for domination by extremists or community polarization.

"We don't advertise a sex education course," said Larry F. Brunswick, superintendent of the Bluffton, Ohio, school district. "We teach it in health, science and home economics." Incorporating it into a variety of courses avoids controversy, he said. "Don't make it into a big issue," he warned administrators.

The key to success, he advised, is to "manage the program well and avoid controversies."

Chapter Two

A Question Of Responsibility: The School's Role In Pregnancy Prevention

When it comes to the delicate issue of teenage sexuality, the role of the public schools has been as confused as a pair of ninth-graders on their first date. The question is, how far should they go?

Schools aren't sure if they can make do with a few superficial discussions about sex, or whether they must prove they have a long-term commitment to modifying students' behavior and, ultimately, stopping them from getting pregnant.

The problem is that adults "deal with adolescent pregnancy, not adolescent sexuality," said Mary Lee Tatum, coordinator of Family Life Education in the Falls Church, Va., public schools. "It's an American trait to deal superficially with an issue and then speak on it profoundly."

School officials, believes Tatum, are no different from most American adults. "We don't see sexuality as child-related. We see it as adult-related. Adolescents have sex because they've been told it's adult behavior and they want to be adults. We have to tell them it's okay to feel sexual" but they shouldn't feel pressure to have sex.

Most schools are afraid to be that frank. Even though teen pregnancy is considered to be, in the words of National Education Association spokesman Howard Carroll, a "super-issue" for schools, educators continue to walk a tightrope between the dual roles of educator and moral guardian.

Sex Ed Programs: Who Has Them And What Are They?

Sex education, in one form or another, has caught on like wildfire. As early as 1971, 55 percent of large school districts were found to offer sex education programs. Eleven years later, a survey of almost 200 large school districts by the Urban Institute found that three out of four districts offered some type of sex education curriculum.

Although most schools offer some kind of sex education programs, the programs have little in common except, perhaps, an aversion to tackling the issue of birth control. Many schools "are providing information about contraception and abstinence, but aren't providing it with a great deal of depth," said Asta-Maria Kenney, associate for policy development at the Alan Guttmacher Institute in Washington, D.C.

Indeed, teens must have far greater access to contraceptives, according to a National Research Council panel. The panel, which is affiliated with the National Academy of Sciences, issued a hard-hitting report in December 1986 that said the "major strategy" in fighting teen pregnancy must be contraception, especially the pill, which it called the "safest and most effective means of birth control."

The panel also endorsed family life and sexuality education and programs to enhance the life options of young people by helping them improve school performance, obtain jobs and identify role models.

Other types of sex education, according to the Urban Institute, run the gamut from a 45-minute lecture on anatomy to a graduated series of courses geared to the age of the participating students. Sometimes sex education is a course by itself, sometimes it's a unit in a larger course and sometimes it's offered as an extracurricular program.

> "Adolescents have sex because they've been told it's adult behavior and they want to be adults. We have to tell them it's okay to feel sexual" but they shouldn't feel pressure to have sex.
> — *Mary Lee Tatum, coordinator of Family Life Education, Falls Church, Va., public schools*

The U.S. General Accounting Office, in a 1986 analysis of the most recent studies on sex education, identified five broad categories of sex education programs, ranging from peer workshops to school-parent programs to full-scale health clinics.

Any attempt to define sex education becomes even more difficult when the different programs' goals are taken into account.

A layperson might expect that a program called "sex education" is intended to prevent unwanted pregnancies. But that's not the case. "We always talk about sex education as a means of preventing pregnancy, but only 40 percent (of districts polled by the Urban Institute) have as their goal the prevention of pregnancy," noted Kenney.

Instead, the Urban Institute found the most popular goal of sex education programs was simply "to promote rational and informed decisionmaking about sexuality," chosen by 94 percent of the 200 districts polled.

Not that schools ignored pregnancy prevention: nearly three quarters included it in their curricula and most devoted at least one class period to it. Viewed as a whole, however, the programs presented the most information on the physiological and interpersonal aspects of sexuality and the least on contraceptives and family planning. That's not necessarily bad. "One has to have very clear objectives. If you have other goals, fine," said Kenney, "but don't expect to reduce teenage pregnancy."

Sex Education: No Stranger To Controversy

Practically from its start, the sex education movement has been awash in controversy, most of it generated by well organized, vocal opponents:

> At the end of the 1960s, fledgling (sex education) programs became the target for political and religious organizations of the Far Right. . . . Opponents tried to cripple programs by using a variety of intimidating techniques: anonymous phone calls to educators, harassment of teachers and administrators at public meetings, law suits against school boards and support for candidates who vowed to abolish programs. Programs in 30 states were attacked. While many programs survived, the atmosphere for further expansion and development was chilled.
>
> The after effects of these attacks are still evident. . . . A majority of students receive some sexuality education in high school, but in-depth discussion of sexual relationships is rarely introduced below the ninth grade. Information at the high school level is generally folded into a required health education curriculum along with education about drugs, alcohol, first aid and nutrition. The emphasis is placed on the physiological facts of reproduction. Information about emotions and feelings, self-esteem, confidence, values and decision-making are often not included. (Susan Wilson, "Creating Family Life Education Programs in the Public Schools," National Association of State Boards of Education, Alexandria, Va., 1985.)

One of the most common arguments against sex education — and one that's been used for more than two decades — is that telling kids about sex encourages them to engage in it. Typical of the argument is this 1984 attack by Sen. Jesse Helms, R-N.C., on Title X of the federal Public Health Service Act, which provides federal support for family planning demonstration projects:

> A distinguished constitutional authority recently said that one and a half billion dollars in the hands of terrorists could not have inflicted the long-term harm to our society that Title X expenditures have. . . . No one can deny the fact that Title X does indeed subsidize teenage sexual activity. It is on the basis

"We've Got To Stop Saying Dumb Things To Teenagers"

Sol Gordon is swinging his arms. He's talking at the top of his voice. And his audience is enthralled.

Gordon, a familiar face in the world of sexuality education, is getting worked up about teenage sexuality and pregnancy.

"We've got to stop saying dumb things to teenagers, like don't have sex until you're married," says Gordon, an author (*Raising a Child Conservatively in a Sexually Permissive World*) and professor. "Less than 5 percent of couples are both virgins when they get married. The Talmud says expect miracles but don't count on them."

Gordon talks in exclamation points. "Sexual intercourse is a health hazard! It's not a good idea! But half of all teens have sex whether we like it or they like it!"

Teachers, Gordon says, need to talk very frankly to teens in words they understand. "We don't tell kids what they want to know. Tell girls how to fight off boys. When the boy says, 'I'll just stay in for a minute," the girl should say, 'What am I, a microwave oven?'"

Gordon believes sex education courses commonly offered in the nation's schools are not really sex education. "We have courses in plumbing—the relentless pursuit of the Fallopian tubes."

And he believes sex education courses must be moral, as distinct from moralistic. The difference? "It's okay to say, 'It's bad to get pregnant as a teen.' It's not okay to say, 'If you do, you'll go to hell.'"

Finally, schools should not worry about being controversial. "If you're not controversial, you're boring."

of this fact that some argue Title X directly and positively increases the incidence of venereal disease, teenage pregnancy, and abortion.

At a minimum, Title X tends to create an atmosphere in which teenage promiscuity is viewed as normal and acceptable conduct and which in turn fosters the very problems we are trying to solve.

While fire-and-brimstone arguments like Helms's certainly would make teachers and school officials (elected school officials, in particular) think twice about launching a sex education program, virtually no research backs up his claims.

Two studies show just the contrary—that sex education programs have little or no influence on teenage sexual activity. Both studies were based on large national surveys and both drew strikingly similar conclusions, even though the surveys were done two years apart and were analyzed by different researchers.

Johns Hopkins University researcher Deborah Anne Dawson, working with data from a 1982 National Survey of Family Growth poll of nearly 2,000 teenage girls, concluded that "exposure to formal sex education appears to have no consistent effect on the subsequent probability that a teenager will have intercourse."

> *Even though teen pregnancy is considered to be a "super-issue" for schools, educators continue to walk a tightrope between the dual roles of educator and moral guardian.*

Dawson compared teenagers who had taken a sex education course with those who hadn't to see if any differences existed in the frequency of sexual activity. She found a few differences, but nothing significant enough to either condemn or condone sex education.

Researchers from Ohio State University's Center for Human Resource Research came to much the same conclusion. Their analysis of 12,000 questionnaires administered to men and women in 1979 and 1986 as part of the National Longitudinal Survey of Work Experience of Youth found factors other than sex education to have the greatest influence on the initiation of intercourse.

Some of those factors, not surprisingly, included church attendance, family background and geographical location. When these factors were accounted for, the impact of a sex education class became slight.

The second prong of the political attack against sex education focuses on what sex education programs should be replaced with, namely, programs that encourage abstinence, not contraception.

"Rather than presuming that teenagers are going to have sex anyway, our collective strategy for combatting teen pregnancy should be similar to the approach we have taken on curbing adolescent drug addiction, alcohol abuse, and smoking—we should encourage teens to say 'no,'" argued a 1986 report by the Family Research Council, a Washington, D.C., think tank.

"To tell teens that premarital sex is neither right nor wrong, conservatives maintain, is to abandon society's moral standards. No responsible teacher, parent, school superintendent or counselor would take a 'neutral approach' to stealing, lying, cheating on exams or violence. Yet, this is precisely what is being done in the area of sexual activity," declared the report.

Life Planning Curriculum: The New Trend

Since sex education programs got under way in the 1960s, there have been few additions to the relatively brief, often anemic, programs that constitute most sex ed offerings.

"Not a whole lot has changed over the past 20 to 25 years . . . the content of sex education programs has not made very strong strides," said Kenney.

The most significant new sex education curriculum came in 1983, when the Center for Population Options (CPO) in Washington, D.C., introduced its "Life Planning Education" program for testing in three school districts. Life Planning differs from traditional sex education approaches in at least three distinct ways: it provides instruction on everything from personal growth to resume writing; it approaches sex education from a strictly economic angle; and (perhaps most important) it is designed to be politically acceptable to communities that would reject a more straightforward program.

The rationale for developing the new program was the documented link between youth unemployment, education and childbearing. Teen mothers, for example, earn about half as much as women who first give birth in their 20s, and both teen mothers and fathers are far more likely to drop out of school than students who don't have children, according to CPO.

"Our program is very palatable to conservative communities" said Jackie Manley, CPO's program associate. "We take all the [sexual] areas and tie them in with employment. The program is oriented toward future planning and that seems to eliminate the problems people have with straight sex education."

But Manley doesn't want to leave the impression that the program

A Question Of Responsibility

was designed strictly to sidestep conservative objections. She believes Life Planning provides the crucial motivational component that's missing from most programs.

"For years we talked about abstaining and contraception, but we didn't follow through because there was no motivational angle — nothing concrete that kids could latch onto." In its simplest terms, the portion of Life Planning that deals with sexuality seeks to show kids the impact pregnancy can have on their education, their careers and their wallets.

Getting pregnant, for example, could make it tough to get a high school diploma, which could make it tough to get a job, which could make it tough to support a child. "We don't ask the question 'Should I have intercourse?'" said Manley, "but instead ask, 'If I have three children, can I have a career?' That seems to take the edge off it."

"By putting sex education in the broader context of planning for futures, the need for sexual responsibility becomes more apparent to teens," says CPO literature. The full Life Planning Education program, which can be taught in brief, self-contained modules or as a semester-long course, consists of three units:

> Teens "are petrified their sexuality will be discovered and would rather risk a pregnancy than have someone see them buying contraceptives or doing some incriminating behavior."
>
> —Jean Hunter, family life education specialist, Alexandria, Va., public schools

- Unit I, "Who Am I?" focuses on self-assessment, personal and family values, and sex role stereotypes. Teenagers examine themselves, their interests and their beliefs. The chapter on stereotypes is designed to combat myths surrounding typical jobs suited for men and women.
- Unit II, "Where Am I Going?" tries to take the information teens learned in Unit I and translate it into possible jobs and careers. A chapter on parenthood looks at the responsibilities of raising a family.
- Unit III, "How Do I Get There?" includes a chapter on sexuality that examines peer pressure, reproductive anatomy and contraceptive methods. An employment chapter tells how to read classified ads and prepare resumes, and describes how parenthood affects people's work.

The Life Planning Education program has become unexpectedly popular among schools dealing with both mainstream and disadvantaged students. "I can't keep up with all the requests we've received. We've probably sent out more than 1,000 curriculum guides in the last year and a half," said Manley.

Like most other sexuality education programs, however, hard data are in short supply when it comes to judging the effectiveness of the curriculum. A pilot program in El Paso, Texas, showed that students had "increased their knowledge" and changed their attitudes about women's career options, but revealed little about changes in sexual behavior or teen pregnancy rates.

The Life Planning Education program, in fact, may leave its mark not as a sex education program but as a new way to help students focus on long-term goals—one of the perennial problems schools face in trying to prevent students from dropping out. The program may also signal the start of a new trend: expanding sex education beyond a one- or two-week session in high school and making it part of a learning program that stretches over all grades.

School-Based Clinics: A Bolder Approach

Just as Life Planning Education represents a new way to attack the teen pregnancy problem academically, school-based clinics represent a new way to attack it medically.

A 1986 count found up to 100 clinics in operation, mostly in urban, disadvantaged schools where teens have health care problems. Getting a fix on the "typical" school-based clinic is hard to do because they are largely a grass-roots phenomenon. They're rarely instigated by school districts, but instead are promoted by concerned citizens and community agencies that form partnerships with school officials.

In some cases, said researcher and former CPO chairwoman Joy Dryfoos, clinics are established as a direct response to alarmingly high teen pregnancy rates. In other cases, they are set up to provide general health care services and later expand into pregnancy care and prevention, in part to avoid political opposition, she said.

"The schools where clinics seem to go are the schools where there are problems and where they need help. These are not suburban areas. These are areas where kids don't have a personal physician," Dryfoos said.

Clinics are a crucial element in preventing pregnancies because teens "are petrified their sexuality will be discovered and would rather risk a pregnancy than have someone see them buying contraceptives or doing some incriminating behavior," said Jean Hunter, a family life education specialist for the Alexandria, Va., public schools. "Teens must be provided with confidential counseling and a safe place to go where insurance is given that no one will find out about their sexual activity."

Agrees Penny Smith, administrator of the Annandale, Va., Women's Center, which operates three free clinics for teens in northern Virginia: "The main reasons teenagers don't use birth control is that it costs too much and isn't available to teenagers. We have eliminated both those reasons."

* * *

Clinics have been blocked in many communities over the issue of birth control. Some clinics dispense contraceptives, some issue prescriptions that can be filled off-campus and some merely provide counseling and referrals.

In nearly all cases, the contraceptive program has survived, although sometimes in a less active form (referrals instead of distribution, for example). That in itself may signal a change in public attitudes toward teen sexuality. "The trend toward school-based clinics is truly remarkable. I frankly would not have thought such a thing possible," said the Guttmacher Institute's Kenney.

"All clinics have to go through a stage of community development," said Dryfoos. "It seems in most cases that opposition peaks when a clinic opens, but goes away over time. Once the parents step in and say they want the services, the controversy dies down."

* * *

Controversy over contraceptives is only one of the roadblocks to clinics. Schools already hard-pressed to find funds and space for regular programs may resist spending money for a program that may be unpopular among some parents.

In Alexandria, Va., where officials in 1986 were considering a proposal for a school-based clinic, money and space are obstacles. "There are some teachers who don't even have their own classroom right now," said Sandra Lindsay, assistant chairwoman of the school board. And even if a portable trailer could be brought in to make space for the clinic, "a government grant or funding from the city would be needed to pay for maintenance of the clinic," she said.

And school officials are always wary when dealing with health issues. "Right now a school nurse has to call a child's parent before she gives the child an aspirin," said Donna Kloch, president of the Alexandria PTA Council. "We're talking about dispensing birth

What Doctors Can Do About Teen Pregnancy

Teachers shouldn't have to go it alone. But many physicians—arguably the best placed to help teens deal with their sexuality—can't handle the responsibility either.

Dr. Robert Johnson, director of adolescent medicine at the University of Medicine and Dentistry of New Jersey in Newark, is one who can. And does.

"As a physician, you have access to adolescents that other people don't have," Johnson said. "I have the opportunity to make a point with them about controlling their sexual habits. My wife is an educator. She calls this time I have with adolescents 'an educable moment,' a time to get a very important point across."

What does Johnson do? "I put up posters and reading material in my waiting room. It's pretty obvious, but many physicians don't do it. Then I ask questions. People ask me, 'How do you get teens to talk about sex?' I tell them, 'Just ask!'

"Just ask, 'Are you sexually active?' If they say yes, then ask, 'Do you use birth control?' If they don't, you must educate them. If they do, you must follow-up to be sure they're using them correctly. There are many misconceptions about birth control. One boy said he and his girlfriend were on the pill. He said he took the pill one month and she took it the next month."

But adolescents, according to Johnson, are "much more intelligent than we think they are. It doesn't make sense to me that once teenagers have babies, they're emancipated, they're expected to support themselves in an adult world, but before, they're not considered intelligent enough to talk about birth control and sex."

Some adolescents "don't want to answer your questions," he said. "In those cases, it's important to leave the door open, to let them know they can call you if they change their minds."

Finally, Johnson said he is "always accused of preaching sex. I have to remind you that most adolescents are not as sexually active as we are led to believe. It's important to remind them that it's not necessary to have sex to be an adult."

control to students without their parents knowing it. That's huge. There will have to be a lot of discussion about it."

* * *

What school officials may fear most is ending up in court, where Chicago school officials found themselves in 1986.

At a clinic in Chicago's DuSable High School, vocal opponents, many from anti-abortion groups, strongly protested the clinic's distribution of contraceptives, bringing the issue to a school board vote in 1985. The board stuck by the clinic by a one-vote margin, in part because of some 300 babies born to DuSable's 1,000 female students, a factor that undoubtedly contributed to the school's 50 percent dropout rate.

Since its 1985 reprieve, the DuSable clinic has taken a number of steps to strengthen its community backing. Before students can use clinic services, their parents must visit the clinic with them and sign a consent form in person.

An open-door policy lets parents visit the clinic any time, and a staff member keeps parents up to date on clinic happenings.

The goal of preventing unwanted pregnancies is embraced by less than half of the programs run by the schools located in the nation's 200 largest cities.

The Chicago clinic was struck again by controversy in 1986, this time by a group of black ministers who filed a lawsuit alleging the clinic was a "calculated, pernicious effort to destroy the very fabric of family life among black parents and their children." The ministers also blasted the Chicago school board for stripping parents of the right to object to the program and for establishing the religion of "secular humanism" in the curriculum.

The ministers charged the clinic has subverted the use of the parental permission form by not telling parents they can let their child use some of the services—such as immunizations and sport physicals—while not letting them use family planning services.

The mere existence of the clinic, maintains the lawsuit, constitutes "proselytization of public school students to adopt and embrace" secular humanism, which the ministers consider to be a religion.

With the suit still pending in late 1986, clinic officials said the clinic has wide community support and has yet to receive a single complaint from a parent. Clinic officials also say that 80 percent of the visits to DuSable are unrelated to contraception and that before receiving contraceptives students must attend a counseling session where they are advised, among other things, to refrain from sex.

* * *

What does the future hold for school-based clinics? Since the first clinic was established in St. Paul, Minn., in 1973, little support for them has existed at higher levels of government. But that may be changing, Dryfoos said. "Schools are beginning to initiate clinics. That's a change. There's an increase in the number of public health departments that are taking the lead."

A 1986 study by CPO's Support Center for School-Based Clinics made the same finding. "A new era in this fledgling movement has begun," declared the report. "Special task forces, school boards, and other governmental bodies are calling for the creation of SBC's (school-based clinics), and state legislatures and state health departments are appropriating funds." Oregon became the first state to launch a clinic program in 1985, earmarking $250,000 to start five pilot programs aimed at reducing sexually transmitted diseases, drug abuse, mental health problems and student pregnancy.

> "A distinguished constitutional authority recently said that one and a half billion dollars in the hands of terrorists could not have inflicted the long-term harm to our society that Title X expenditures have."
> —Sen. Jesse Helms, R-N.C.

Oregon law bars the pilot program from paying for contraceptive distribution or abortion counseling—a common restriction proposed by state-level task forces that are considering starting school-based clinic programs, according to the center.

Are the clinics effective in reducing teen pregnancy? Administrators of the St. Paul clinics say their program has worked. The percentage of female students receiving family planning services at the district's three clinics has risen from zero to 35 percent. The rates of students who stay on contraceptives for one year and two years are 93 percent and 82 percent at the two oldest sites. And as a result of the counseling and family planning services, say St. Paul administrators, 80 percent of student mothers now remain in school and only 1.4 percent of adolescent mothers who stay in school have a repeat pregnancy within two years.

But those gains do not come without a price. Nationally, it costs an estimated $25,000 to $250,000 annually to run the clinic—

about $100 to $124 per student patient. And the National Research Council, in a December 1986 report, said the St. Paul clinics are the only one nationwide to demonstrate "significant reduction" in the number of repeat pregnancies. Of the teenage mothers who stayed in school and received contraceptive services from the St. Paul clinics between 1974 and 1980, only 1.3 percent experienced a repeat pregnancy one year after birth, compared with 18 percent or higher nationally.

* * *

All in all, most schools play a confused role, giving students little hard advice one way or another when it comes to the issue of sexual activity. In many respects, this approach bears an uncanny resemblance to sex education programs Sweden abandoned in the 1970s because they did little to help the student.

The position of Sweden's early sex education program "was that of sexual abstinence throughout adolescence. However, as the custom of 'going steady' (including, at times, a sexual relationship), became more common among Swedish teenagers . . . adherence to this standard placed the teacher in an untenable situation," wrote Carl Gustaf Boethius, former secretary of the Swedish commission that established a sex education manual issued to teachers in 1977.

"If the teacher simply enunciated the standard of teenage abstinence, it meant that he or she was unable to bring up for discussion the real issues confronting a growing body of students. As a result, teaching became one-sided, emphasizing the biological aspects of sexual relationships and ignoring their ethical and psychological dimensions," Boethius wrote.

"In addition, a pedagogical concept had been introduced into Swedish teaching philosophy, which asserted that for democratic reasons, all teaching in the humanities should be morally neutral and value-free. The resulting sex education that students received tended not to be of great usefulness to them, and it provided them with little real guidance in their lives."

Caught between a continuing teenage pregnancy problem and the moral outrage of politicians and others, it's no wonder that most American sex education programs have to approach sexuality and contraception obliquely, touching on them only briefly before returning to the safer grounds of anatomical drawings and biological events.

The question that now must be answered is whether these programs—particularly in their often watered down states—do anything to combat the crisis of teen pregnancy.

Do The Programs Work?

Assuming schools do have a role in combatting teen pregnancy, and assuming that role includes sex education, family planning, and even health care and contraceptive services, educators must still ask the big question: does it all do any good?

When you ask that question of the advocates of teen sexuality programs, you get some surprising answers:

- "If your one objective is to reduce teen pregnancy, you're setting yourself up for failure. A sex education program is not going to do that. I'm convinced of it." —Jackie Manley, program associate, Center for Population Options

- "Until we get the parents, the community, and the churches involved, we won't be successful (at reducing teen pregnancy). Even then, it's going to take a number of years before we'll be able to see something. You can't make an impact in just two weeks of classes." —Nina Jackson, director of adolescent pregnancy programs, Fort Worth, Texas, schools

> *"Rather than presuming that teenagers are going to have sex anyway, our collective strategy for combatting teen pregnancy should be similar to the approach we have taken on curbing adolescent drug addiction, alcohol abuse, and smoking—we should encourage teens to say 'no.'"*
> *—Family Research Council, Washington, D.C.*

- "Comprehensive programs, despite their many virtues, are not the magic bullets that will solve the problems associated with unintended teen pregnancy and parenthood. Nor should be they expected to do so." —Richard Weatherley, researcher, University of Washington School of Social Work

The major argument against the sex education movement is glaring: it hasn't made a statistical dent in the teen pregnancy rate. That rate stood at 9.5 percent in 1972, but rose to 10.1 percent in just under 10 years. Even more damning, argues Stan Weed, director of the Institute for Research and Evaluation, a Salt Lake City think tank, is the massive rise in teenage abortions—from 190,000 to 400,000 over the same period. "Apparently the [sex education] programs were more effective at convincing teens to avoid birth than to avoid pregnancy."

Those figures, however, tell just part of the complicated numerical picture. Looked at from a different perspective, it can be said that sex education programs held back what could have been an even larger wave of pregnancies. While the rate of teen sexual activity rose by two-thirds in the 1970s, for example, the pregnancy rate increased by only 12.5 percent, according to the Guttmacher Institute. The reason? Perhaps, says the institute, because the use of contraceptives increased by 35 percent.

While the statistics paint a picture of a half-full, half-empty glass, it seems hardly fair to expect America's patchwork web of locally run sex education programs to make a major impact on national statistical rates.

"When you say sex education doesn't work, I don't know if we've ever had a real long-term K-12 program to measure. How do we know it doesn't work? I don't think there's any community that's gone at it full steam," said Manley. "If you're measuring a semester course in the life of a teen-age sophomore, you're not going to make a difference."

Data from the national polls analyzed by researchers at Johns Hopkins and Ohio State universities bear out Manley's point. Students who had taken sex education courses were neither more or less likely to become pregnant, in the long run, than teenagers who hadn't taken sex education courses.

To get a better view of the teen pregnancy problem, some researchers

> *"The main reasons teenagers don't use birth control are that it costs too much and isn't available to teenagers. We have eliminated both those reasons."*
>
> *—Penny Smith, administrator, Annandale, Va., Women's Center*

have taken a hard look at specific types of programs, such as school clinics. The best evidence to date that sex education can work comes from a study of a broad program in Baltimore that provided students with sexuality and contraceptive information, individual and group counseling, and medical and contraceptive services over three years.

Comparing students in the program schools with students in other Baltimore schools, researchers found major differences in age of first intercourse, use of contraceptives and overall pregnancy rates. The pregnancy rate of teenagers in the two junior and two senior high schools that had the comprehensive program dropped by 22 percent after 20 months of exposure to the program, compared to a 39 percent increase in the pregnancy rate of non-program students.

"In the face of rising rates in many U.S. cities, the marked reduction in pregnancy demonstrated here is welcomed," said a group of Johns Hopkins researchers who studied the program.

Critics have tried to discredit the Baltimore results, saying

Want To Avoid Teen Pregnancy? Move To North Dakota

Teen pregnancy is most likely to happen in Nevada and least likely to happen in North Dakota, according to a major study by the Alan Guttmacher Institute, a family planning research group.

Using 1980 statistics—the most recent available—the 1986 study projected teen pregnancy rates for individual states, and found large differences among them. The teen pregnancy rate (made up of births, abortions and miscarriages to girls 15 to 19) for the United States as a whole in 1980 was 111 per 1,000.

North Dakota had the lowest rate, with 75 per 1,000, followed by Minnesota with 77 per 1,000.

Differences among states were not easy to explain, said Jane Murray, a spokeswoman for the institute. Densely settled states with widespread poverty and fluctuating populations tended to have more pregnant teens than less populated states such as Iowa, Minnesota and the Dakotas.

In Nevada, the state with the highest rate of teen pregnancy, 144 teenage girls of every 1,000 get pregnant.

In most states, the majority of pregnant teens elected to keep their babies rather than get abortions. This was particularly true in Southern states. In Mississippi, for example, with a high teenage pregnancy rate of 125 out of 1,000, an estimated 81 girls out of every 1,000 give birth.

In California, with the second highest teen pregnancy rate in the nation, 140 girls out of every 1,000 get pregnant, and 53 out of 1,000 give birth.

For a copy of the study, contact the Alan Guttmacher Institute, 111 Fifth Ave., New York, N.Y. 10003, (212)254-5656.

researchers couldn't take into account the differences between the program and non-program schools or track students who dropped out of school. The team of Hopkins researchers, led by Laurie Zabin, concedes that student mobility is always a problem in such studies, but says the large differences uncovered are strong enough to be statistically significant.

In the end, policymakers can choose from a welter of statistics — calling programs a failure or a success depending on how they interpret the figures.

But policymakers also should keep a sense of perspective about programs in the schools. After all, the message that sex is exciting and glamorous dominates the national media. Sex is used to sell everything from blue jeans to bubble gum — a cultural onslaught school officials certainly can't reverse with a one-semester course. As educators, schools can help students better understand their bodies, their relationships and their futures, but if they want to stop the epidemic of teen pregnancies, they need — and deserve — the help of the entire community.

In addition, say some experts, many poor teens actually believe they benefit from an early pregnancy because they become eligible for welfare.

"Often, a career or a middle class life are not options to these poor girls who become teen mothers anyway," said Mary Jo Bane, executive deputy commissioner of the New York State Department of Social Services.

In New York, state officials tried cutting back on benefits to force teen mothers to find other means of support. It didn't work, said Bane, who believes welfare must provide more incentive to work.

William J. Wilson, chairman of the University of Chicago sociology department, refutes the view that welfare causes teen pregnancy. Instead, he thinks the problem is directly related to the changing labor status of young black males. Their low economic status and joblessness work against the formation of families, Wilson said.

Where Do We Go From Here?

While America's hit-or-miss approach to establishing sex education programs has produced few good results, the tale isn't the same in other countries. If we look at other Western nations similar to the United States, a startling fact stands out: the pregnancy and abortion rates of American teens are twice as high as those of any similar country.

In the Netherlands, 14 out of every 1,000 women ages 15 to 19 becomes pregnant. In Sweden the figure is 35, in France 43, and in Great Britain 45. In America, the comparable figure is 96. "Even more striking," said a report by Alan Guttmacher Institute researchers, "is that the abortion rate alone in the United States is as high, or higher than, the overall teenage pregnancy rate in any of the other" six countries studied.

The huge difference is not explained by differences in sexual activity; Swedish teens, for example, are more sexually active than U.S. youths and teens in the Netherlands have about the same rate of sexual activity as U.S. teens. The difference is instead explained by contraceptive use. American teens had the lowest level of contraceptive use, and when U.S. teens did use contraceptives, they tended to use less effective methods than did European and Canadian teens.

Although adult policymakers may never be able to reach inside a teen's mind to discover the real reasons behind contraceptive use, the Guttmacher study by Elise Jones found two major differences between the United States and foreign nations. The first was the open commitment of foreign governments to put contraceptives in the hands of teens. The second difference was harder to define, but no less tangible, and goes to the heart of America's ambivalent attitudes toward sex.

> *"Our program is very palatable to conservative communities. We take all the [sexual] areas and tie them in with employment. The program is oriented toward future planning and that seems to eliminate the problems people have with straight sex education."*
> *—Jackie Manley, Center for Population Options*

"In the United States, sex tends to be treated as a special topic, and there is much ambivalence: Sex is romantic but also sinful and dirty; it is flaunted but also something to be hidden. This is less true in several European countries, where matter-of-fact attitudes seem to be more prevalent," said Jones.

"I don't think our society recognizes adolescents as human beings," added Manley. "In other countries, sexuality is part of a person's personality from birth. Sexuality is considered positively, and society will talk about it. In the U.S., people have the wrong idea about it. We're not just talking about intercourse. We're talking about part of the human being—being male, being female."

The European countries also make information about sexuality and birth control more available to youngsters than does the United

States. Sweden's sex education program is perhaps the broadest, starting with six- and seven-year-olds. The discussion with young children takes an unusual tack. Young children can be told, said former Swedish official Boethius, that "all children have the right to be wanted at birth, so parents should wait until they can take care of a child before they decide to have a baby (small children very much like hearing this idea)."

By the time the curriculum runs its course at the high school level, several ethical principles should have been instilled in Swedish students, among them: psychological pressure and the use of physical force in any context are violations of personal freedoms; sexuality as part of a personal relationship involves more than casual sex; sexual fidelity in a permanent relationship is a duty; and men and women must be held to the same standards of sexual morality.

"Children who are instilled with a serious sense of sexual responsibility at an early age are not likely to account for a large number of unwanted pregnancies and abortions," said Boethius.

"The trend toward school-based clinics is truly remarkable. I frankly would not have thought such a thing possible."
—*Asta-Maria Kenney, associate for policy development, Alan Guttmacher Institute*

In contrast to the Swedish attitude toward adolescent sex, consider the perplexing world in which Jones believes American teens are trapped: "American teenagers seem to have inherited the worst of all possible worlds. . . . Movies, music, radio and TV tell them that sex is romantic, exciting, titillating; premarital sex and cohabitation are visible ways of life among the adults they see and hear about; their own parents or their parents' friends are likely to be divorced or separated but involved in sexual relationships.

"Yet, at the same time, young people get the message good girls should say no. Almost nothing that they see or hear about sex informs them about contraception or the importance of avoiding pregnancy. . . . Such messages lead to an ambivalence about sex that stifles communication and exposes young people to increased risk of pregnancy, out-of-wedlock births and abortions."

Chapter Three

After The Fact:
Helping Pregnant And Parenting Teens

While controversy swirls around programs to prevent teen pregnancy, programs aimed at helping the pregnant and parenting teenager have received relatively little attention.

When it comes to the schools, the reasons for neglect are somewhat obvious. The role of the schools, after all, is education. And a program that provides prenatal health services, family counseling and day care stretches the boundaries of a school's mission.

"A lot of school leaders feel they're not in the social services business, they're in the education business," said Sharon Rodine, director of the National Organization on Adolescent Pregnancy and Parenting in Reston, Va. And some schools, she said, simply "say they don't have pregnant kids. That's because they push them out early and don't provide any services."

In other instances, a school's objections to pregnancy programs are the same as its objections to sex education programs: bringing the problem into the open will only encourage more of the same behavior. "Many people [in schools] don't like working with pregnant teens. Some consider it to be like a contagious disease; if you have one in, more will be coming," said Ruth Gordon, a senior policy analyst at the Child Welfare League in Washington, D.C.

A University of Washington study of 10 teen pregnancy programs drew a similar conclusion. "Helping pregnant adolescents is often considered an unpopular cause," said the 1983 survey, headed by Richard Weatherley. "While such negative views were more pervasive and more intensely expressed in some areas than in others, they were reported in every one of the study sites."

Indeed, "the difficulty in what we're doing," said Nabers Cabaniss, director of the U.S. Office of Adolescent Pregnancy Programs, "is that we're serving pregnant teens and teen parents. The debate usually centers around prevention."

Program Choices

Despite the uphill struggle, experts agree that the number of programs to help teenage mothers stay in school and give birth to healthy children is on the rise, thanks largely to concerned community groups. Although national statistics on the number and types of pregnancy care programs are not available, Rodine believes most are started by community groups concerned over high pregnancy rates and poor infant health.

The groups often evolve into public-private coalitions or become government-supported task forces, she said. Schools are usually not the agency that gets the ball rolling, but become involved when approached by an outside agency.

The programs are run by a diverse range of agencies—from public schools to the YWCA—and offer an equally diverse range of services. Before the 1970s, programs for pregnant teens were much narrower and simpler. "It used to be that pregnant girls went to maternity residences, but all that has changed dramatically, and now all types of services are being offered," said Cabaniss.

Current services fall into four broad categories, according to a 1986 U.S. General Accounting Office study: prenatal and infant health care; residential care for pregnant teens; alternative schools that provide academic instruction at home or in separate school buildings; and comprehensive programs that provide academic, medical and counseling services.

* * *

What role do the schools play? Some provide nearly all of the above services through an alternative school where the teen can also receive regular classroom instruction. Some schools operate on-campus health clinics that provide health care services, and some merely allow teenagers greater schedule flexibility so they can split their day between their regular classes and attendance at a special school for pregnant and parenting students. In some states, pregnancy is considered a disability and thus comes under handicapped education programs, qualifying the pregnant for special transportation and education services.

Given the broad range of services involved, one might wonder why the schools care to get involved in such programs to begin with. One overriding factor is that pregnancy is the leading reason why female students drop out of school—more than half of all pregnant teens leave school prematurely, and nearly one out of every 10 teenage girls over 14 gets pregnant. The children these mothers give birth to often have health problems and learning disorders, causing even more work for schools when they enter the public education system.

Whether a pregnancy and parenting program succeeds, however, usually depends on factors over which the school has little control, such as the staff's enthusiasm. "The key ingredient is the staff.

There are a lot of subjective factors, but when you get right down to it, it's who does what that counts," said Cabaniss.

Another crucial ingredient schools lack is control over the quality of community health care services. Schools aren't usually in the business of helping pregnant teens, and require the help of community agencies to get their programs off the ground. If the town lacks a solid program for pregnancy care, the Weatherley study found, schools probably won't be able to establish one on their own.

Two Proven Approaches

Just because pregnancy programs are tough to establish doesn't mean there are no success stories. One such success is the New Futures School (NFS) run by the Albuquerque public school system. Helping young women become good mothers, reducing low-weight births and keeping down the number of welfare recipients are not usually the goals of a public school, but NFS has taken on those and other tasks without complaint.

The 441-student middle and high school has tackled the problems caused by teen pregnancy by establishing an alternative program for pregnant teens that offers services ranging from pre natal health care to job counseling to day care. The programs, said Principal Caroline Gaston, have resulted in a 92 percent graduation rate for pregnant teens and teen mothers, a one-year repeat pregnancy rate of 6 percent to 8 percent, compared to a national rate of 18 percent to 25 percent, and a nearly 50 percent reduction in the expected number of low-weight births.

Thanks to the Albuquerque teen parenting program, "We believe that we have better parents and more self-assured young women."
— *Caroline Gaston, principal, New Futures Schools, Albuquerque, N.M.*

"We believe that we have better parents and more self-assured young women," said Gaston, who believes the school succeeds because it puts all the pieces of the pregnancy puzzle together under one roof. "We're fairly rare in that we provide all types of services. But those services together provide the right kind of caring environment so that they [students] can believe in themselves. I think that's the most important thing."

NFS offers its services to any pregnant teen, and allows teens to enroll at any time during the school year. One-third of the students are 15 years old and younger and 40 percent have dropped out

before enrolling in NFS. The school's services fall into four basic areas:
1. Education courses leading to a high school diploma or basic skills classes leading toward an equivalency degree. NFS also offers accredited classes in prenatal care, child development and parenting.
2. Medical care through on-site services, home visits, health assessments for mothers and children, and nutrition instruction.
3. Counseling and social services, including weekly group sessions, counseling for families and teen fathers, adoption counseling and referrals to local social service agencies.
4. On-campus child care services for children in three different age groups that do double duty as "learning labs" for future mothers.

The school can't provide all those services itself, said Gaston, but relies on assistance from local, state and federal agencies, including the local public health department, the University of New Mexico School of Medicine, and the U.S. Women, Infant and Children's Nutritional Program.

In fact, community groups got NFS off the ground to begin with, approaching the school with their proposal to launch an alternative school to combat the city's teen pregnancy problem. "It was tough at first, but the fact that it started out as a community project helped," said Gaston.

* * *

The support of the community was also crucial in starting the New Lives program in Fort Worth, Texas, which began in the early 1970s, about the same time NFS was launched in Albuquerque.

Like NFS, the New Lives program consists of a separate school for pregnant and parenting mothers run by the public school system. It offers day care, medical care and social services, in addition to conventional education courses.

While sex education programs have run into heated opposition in the conservative Texas town, the New Lives program has been operating with little controversy. "People are not upset about doing something for a kid once she's pregnant," said Nina Jackson, director of adolescent pregnancy services for the public schools.

The biggest problem Fort Worth's ambitious program faces is not community opposition, but lack of funds. The comprehensive alternative school and a day care center for student mothers have about exhausted their school district funds and must rely on community donations for expansion. But there's good news: 30 residents formed a community-based nonprofit corporation to help raise the needed funds.

"Most of the programs have been funded through the community. They put the icing on the cake because they provide the funds. You've got to have the community's support. It's just too expensive otherwise," Jackson said.

Jackson is a strong advocate of alternative schools for teen mothers, arguing that it's not only cheaper than a decentralized program (services don't have to be duplicated in the city's 12 high schools and 17 middle schools), but also provides more support for struggling students. "In our school everybody is on the same wavelength. We really provide a nurturing atmosphere."

Another strong plus for the program, said Jackson, is the day care center for student mothers. "We use the day care center as a carrot to get them [students] involved" in the alternative school's education programs.

In the future, Jackson hopes New Lives will be able to offer counseling for teen fathers, help with landing a job, and family planning services. Teens can get family planning assistance at local hospitals, said Jackson, but it's been too controversial for the schools to get involved with as yet.

Although Jackson wants to do more, she also believes that no single program — no matter how comprehensive — is going to solve the teen pregnancy problem. "Programs really kill themselves when they try to be everything. Schools can only affect one level." The available research, what little there is, tends to bear out Jackson's statement.

Odds On Success

An unwanted teen pregnancy is already perceived as the sign of one failure, be it by the student, the school or the family, but it's hardly cause to abandon the mother-to-be. Without a high school diploma, the chance to get a good job and the knowledge to plan a family, so the reasoning goes, a teen mother will be likely to get pregnant again.

The most ambitious efforts to tackle this problem are the so-called "comprehensive" programs that bring together a wide range of community resources. But whether such a program can successfully be put together in the first place is a difficult question to answer, and whether it will work is not at all certain. Weatherley's research, for example, identified four hurdles such programs have to clear: lack of money; lack of existing medical and social services;

political opposition; and overambitious program goals.

Overly ambitious goals, for instance, may have doomed some programs from the start. "In claims reminiscent of those made for the patent medicine nostrums of the 19th century, it was argued that that teenage pregnancy services would combat child abuse, crime, youth unemployment, sexual abuse, infant mortality, mental retardation, birth defects, drug abuse. . . . It is not surprising that many of them fall short of meeting the more modest goals, let alone of solving complex social problems," Weatherley said.

Although Weatherley didn't assess the actual outcome of the programs, he did make a good guess that any impact would be small. The evidence suggests "that many of the ill effects associated with adolescent pregnancy are rooted in poverty, a condition not explicitly addressed by any of the programs and services. In reality, the programs are offered in the mode of crisis intervention: They are short-term and involve little or no follow-up."

* * *

More precise evidence of effectiveness is found in a study of Project Redirection, a comprehensive program that operated in four cities from 1980 to 1983. The program wasn't based in schools, but it had the same goals as school-based programs. Sponsored by the Ford Foundation and the U.S. Department of Labor, the program either offered directly or referred pregnant teens to a variety of health, education and job counseling services.

The program included an individual plan for each student that coordinated services from throughout the community. It provided personal role models for the students through community volunteers, arranged peer-group support meetings and provided other services, including employment and medical counseling.

A close study of girls who were enrolled in the program for about one year (longer than most other programs), turned up both good and bad news. Program participants were more likely to be in school or to graduate from school than nonparticipants and were significantly less likely to become pregnant again, reported researchers Denise Polit and Janet Kahn of Humanalysis Inc. and the American Institutes for Research, respectively.

The bad news? Just two years after leaving the program, those gains faded away to insignificance. During the first year of the study, for example, 14 percent of the program teenagers had a repeat pregnancy, compared to 22 percent of the control group. Two years into the study, and about one year after leaving the program,

45 percent of the students in the special program had experienced a repeat pregnancy, compared to 49 percent of the control group — an insignificant difference, said the researchers.

The results were much the same when it came to education. After one year, 56 percent of the program students were in class or had graduated, compared to 49 percent of the control group. But after two years, the figure for both groups was the same: 43 percent. Virtually the same story was found when looking at the percentage of teens who had managed to hold a job during the study period.

The researchers say they offer educators, and others, a "challenge of enormous proportions. The difficult task that remains is to design more powerful treatments that serve less as an interruption and more as a true opportunity for new directions and life options."

Case Studies

Case Study #1

SEXUALITY EDUCATION AND COUNSELING PROGRAM

Program: Teen Choice, New York City public schools

Summary: Teen Choice is an independent sexuality education and counseling program operated in seven New York City public schools by the 157-year-old Inwood House, one of the nation's oldest homes for unwed mothers.

Contacts: 1. Mindy Stern, Teen Choice program director, Inwood House, 320 E. 82nd St., New York, N.Y. 10028, (212)861-4400
2. Linda Marks, assistant principal, Louis D. Brandeis High School, 145 W. 84th St., New York, N.Y. 10024, (212)799-0300, extension 5
3. Joanne Malcy, social worker, Wadleigh Junior High School, 215 W. 114th St., New York, N.Y. 10026, (212)678-2869

It is Tuesday. The 11 a.m. bell announces class has begun and the ninth grade girls in Joanne Malcy's room at Wadleigh Junior High School in West Harlem are playing with a radio dial, scanning the airwaves to find "Papa, Don't Preach," a song in which rock queen Madonna sings of an unwed teen's decision to keep her unborn baby.

The song has stirred controversy among groups concerned that it glamourizes teen pregnancy, but in this group it is stirring a different kind of debate.

This is Teen Choice, a sexuality education and counseling program conducted in seven New York City schools by the 157-year-old Inwood House, one of the nation's oldest homes for unwed mothers. On this day Malcy, Wadleigh's Teen Choice counselor, is using Madonna's position as a role model for the young to get the girls to think about pregnancy.

"The song says she knows she'll have to sacrifice. What kind of sacrifices do you think she'll have to make?" Malcy asks the group.

"She might not have enough money to raise a child."

"Maybe she'll have problems with school."

"The boy, he won't stay with her to help raise the child."

Members of the group note that the song is really just a song, something Madonna probably recorded because she expected it to be a hit. Madonna, one girl notes, has no children and did not marry until she was in her mid-20s. Malcy does not let the revelation pass lightly.

"In a way," she tells the group, "Madonna is a very good example of a young woman who has done a lot for herself. She's trying to have control over her career."

* * *

Control over one's career, control over one's life, control over one's body. These issues are stressed repeatedly in the Teen Choice program in New York City, a city where, according to the most recently available statistics, 32,970 girls up to age 19 became pregnant in 1982: 1,200 of them were younger than age 15.

> *"The parents have always been very positive about the program. That's 99 percent of the battle."*
> *— Brandeis High School Principal Murray Cohen*

Teen Choice was founded in 1978 after a public school guidance counselor approached Inwood House. "She said she was overwhelmed with pregnant girls and asked if we couldn't send her a counselor to do some preventive work. That was the beginning," said Teen Choice Program Director Mindy Stern.

Since that beginning, the program has been highlighted on the MacNeil-Lehrer Report, cited in two Children's Defense Fund publications as one of several programs in the nation that help prevent adolescent pregnancy, and has served as a model for other in-school programs aimed at reducing teen pregnancy rates.

An effort to quantify the impact of the program is under way, with the help of the William T. Grant Foundation, a national organization that funds adolescent psychological research. John Gibson, a doctoral candidate at Columbia University's School of Social Work, in 1983 began to conduct a longitudinal study of 804 students to determine the program's impact on their behavior and attitudes toward sex. School officials who have worked with the program say they don't need the results, due in spring 1987, to know that Teen Choice is effective.

"I just know the success ratio they've had has been phenomenal," said Jerry Gotkin, a former attendance supervisor at Brandeis High

Sexuality Education and Counseling Program

School on Manhattan's Upper West Side, one of the first schools to use the Teen Choice program.

He cites cases of pregnant girls who, after being referred to the program, received support services that let them stay in school through the pregnancy and return after their children were born.

"The parents have always been very positive about the program," said Brandeis Principal Murray Cohen. "That's 99 percent of the battle."

In its eight years of operation, Stern said, "not one word" of controversy has hit the program.

"We're in schools in very poor neighborhoods. They need all the help they can get and they know we're here to help them," she said.

"We work only with kids in the schools where we have been invited to offer the service and where we get the support that we need," said Stern. "We're in seven schools and we return to those same seven schools year after year, although many others have requested our assistance." Lack of money and fears that expanding Teen Choice beyond high-risk schools might dilute the program have kept the program to the seven schools.

While the program is geared toward encouraging teens to delay having sex, the question, "Will I or won't I?" still comes up and it often comes to the counselors in the form of a girl seeking information on birth control.

Teen Choice counselors work on-site at the schools. All hold masters' degrees in social work and have experience as counselors in reproductive issues or mental health.

"They have to be very experienced before we hire them because essentially what we're doing is sending them out completely on their own in a host setting. I really think it's that professionalism that makes this program so different from many others. We are not relying on volunteers. If they aren't involved with reproductive health care or adolescent mental health they aren't considered for the job," said Stern.

Counselors, when invited, make large group presentations on sex education to classes. They are regularly invited to classes as varied as English literature and computer science. They work closely with gym teachers, recruiting students from the physical education class to attend the once-a-week Teen Choice group discussion session and they offer one-on-one counseling for students who seek it.

Because Teen Choice operates as a counseling service, not as a clinic, the counselors do not dispense birth control but will inform students about birth control and abortions when asked.

"You go into a classroom and you reach everyone who is there that day and hopefully you ignite a spark," said Stern.

But, while the program encourages teens to delay having sex, the question of "Will I or won't I?" still comes up, and it often comes to the counselors in the form of a girl seeking information on birth control. When it does, the counselors schedule one-on-one sessions to explore such issues as whether sex will be satisfying to the girl or whether she is contemplating having sex because she is being pressured by boys or peers.

> *"You go into a classroom and you reach everyone who is there that day and hopefully you ignite a spark."*
> — Mindy Stern, program director, Teen Choice

"There are several things that have to go on when a girl comes and asks for birth control," said Stern. "We try to help them to gain insight into their own behavior." The process is called "option counseling."

Sources for birth control are given when it becomes obvious that the girl plans to have sex — with or without birth control. A similar process takes place if a girl turns to a counselor for advice on an abortion.

"Whether we favor it or not is really irrelevant," said Dominique Moyse-Steinberg, a Teen Choice counselor at Brandeis. "What's really important is option counseling [to ensure] that what is done is done of her own free will."

"I think it's always advantageous to a school to hook up to an agency to provide this type of service," said Stern.

She points to a number of advantages:

1. Schools rarely have the resources — financial or professional — to provide teens with in-depth, accurate information about sexuality and, when needed, to connect them with a network of support services that can help pregnant teens stay in school.

2. Students do not view the counselors as an arm of the school administration and are more likely to bring problems to their attention.

3. Independent counselors can deliver a professional service tailored to the needs of teens without having to deal with issues of seniority, community politics and bureaucratic structures that can plague school-initiated efforts.

"When you're in a setting like this, when you're not funded, when you're not staffed, when you're handling all the issues that face an inner-city school, you need a program like this," said Linda Marks, assistant principal in charge of guidance at Brandeis.

"I imagine you can say with certainty that along the line they've saved many lives," she added. "Not only the lives of the students they've helped but also of their children because, among other things, they teach good parenting. It helps to have the program in the building. We know from experience the students would not go if they were on the outside unless you physically took them by the hand. All New York City high schools, all inner-city schools, need a Teen Choice."

Moyse-Steinberg believes Teen Choice makes a difference, because whether or not teens actually change their behavior "at least they will have a couple of things they've never had before. They will have a lot of information. They will have heard someone talk about things they've never heard talked about before. They've learned about taking responsibility for their own behavior and they know they have a place that's safe that they can come to in a crisis."

This case study was researched and written by Carol Ellison, a former education writer for the Cincinnati Post who is now a freelance writer based in New Jersey.

Case Study #2

MINI SCHOOLS FOR PREGNANT TEENS

Program: Pregnant Adolescent Continuing Education program (PACE), Minneapolis School District

Summary: PACE provides basic education for pregnant teens in a "school within a school" setting. The district spends $4,139 annually on each girl in PACE; most of the funding comes from property taxes, regular state aid to school districts and special education money. The courses, which are specially designed for pregnant students, focus on such things as prenatal nutrition and personal finances.

Contacts: 1. Rebecca Strandlund, coordinator, PACE, Northeast Junior High School, 2955 NE Hayes St., Minneapolis, Minn. 55418, (612)627-3053
2. William Phillips, deputy superintendent, Minneapolis School District, 807 NE Broadway, Minneapolis, Minn. 55413, (612)627-2012
3. Edith Garmezy, early organizer and principal, PACE, 5115 Lake Ridge Road, Edina, Minn. 55436, (612)938-3082

Two months before she was to begin her junior year, Sheri Malrick learned she was pregnant. She says administrators of her suburban Minneapolis school suggested she stay home during the last three months of her pregnancy and finish courses with the help of a tutor.

"I didn't want to do that," said Malrick, who is 16. "I'd feel like a prisoner. I wouldn't want to be home and have a question about something and wait for the tutor to come." Moreover, Malrick wanted to avoid the stares and snickers she expected from fellow students while attending school during the early months of her pregnancy.

So she left her mother's suburban home and moved in with her aunt in Minneapolis to qualify for that city's mini-school for pregnant students. Since its founding in 1968, the Minneapolis School District's Pregnant Adolescent Continuing Education program

(PACE) has proven to be a magnet for girls who have considered dropping out of school rather than sitting in regular classrooms while pregnant.

About 200 girls—two-thirds of all pregnant students in the Minneapolis district—attend PACE in a typical year. At any time, 70 to 100 girls attend the five classrooms located in the basement of a junior high school. The district spends $4,139 annually on each girl in PACE, about 30 percent more than the average cost of educating its secondary school students. Most of the funding comes from property taxes, regular state aid to school districts and special education money.

Pregnant students in Minneapolis have the option of staying in their regular schools. But PACE draws most girls by offering a curriculum, staff and atmosphere unique in the school district. The nine-person staff includes a social worker and counselor specializing in problems of pregnant adolescents. All teachers are certified to teach special education students, who often comprise a significant part of the enrollment. Classes on prenatal nutrition and personal finance for single mothers supplement regular courses in math, science, English and social studies for grades 7 through 12.

Sheri Malrick wanted to avoid the stares and snickers she expected from fellow students while attending school during the early months of her pregnancy.

Classes serve students from ages 12 to 20, including a half-dozen refugees from Laos who speak little English. Many students come from broken homes or poor families. The five full-time teachers must be flexible and resourceful to reach students with vast differences in ability in the same room.

Inez Todd, an energetic woman with a forceful voice, moves from desk to desk to give individual attention in teaching civics, American history, government and world history to 11 students in four grade levels. Five girls from Laos sit on one side of the room, their faces expressionless, as Todd talks about South Africa, government propaganda and war. An interpreter translates the lesson for them. Making the point that words can be misused, Todd asks the Laotian students if they have heard of "yellow rain." Blank stares. The interpreter tells them that the "rain" was actually dangerous chemicals sprayed in Southeast Asia during the Vietnam War.

Down the hall, Margaret Kremers teaches parenting, nutrition and hygiene to seven girls in a class adorned with posters advocating balanced diets. She shows a movie on venereal disease and asks students about their eating habits.

"Did you eat any breakfast?" she asks one girl, who shakes her head shyly. Kremers smiles and says, "Your baby's going to get hungry. You should eat breakfast. It's real important that your baby has food. It's important for its teeth to grow and for its brain to grow. You want to have a smart kid, don't you?"

Minneapolis began its mini-school program in a school since torn down. It moved to its current location in 1978. The program has thrived, although its proponents and administrators were apprehensive in the early years.

"You didn't talk about pregnancy of students in those days," said Edith Garmezy, a driving force behind the school in its fledgling years and one of its first principals. "I remember talking with an associate superintendent who said this would be considered a communist plot. You had people who felt that pregnant girls should suffer." But real opposition never materialized. School officials avoided making a splash when they launched the program and kept a low profile until attitudes changed.

PACE has proven to be a magnet for girls who have considered dropping out of school rather than sitting in regular classrooms while pregnant.

Administrators of other school districts who want to establish a mini-school should do their homework about the frequency of student pregnancy in their schools, prepare a sales pitch for the community and arrange financing for at least five years, advises PACE coordinator Rebecca Strandlund.

"I'd certainly try to survey young women to find out how many would like it (a mini-school) if they were pregnant, and how many pregnancies there are," Strandlund said. "I think you'd need a big commitment. You're running separate food service, separate transportation. We're the only school that uses buses to pick up kids at their doors. You have to do that or the students won't come."

School districts such as Minneapolis, which experienced declining enrollment during the 1970s and early 1980s, may be able to use a vacant wing or floor for a pregnancy mini school. But administrators may still have to adjust to tight quarters. "Our problems include running a phys. ed. class in half of the English room, having the 'lunchroom' in the hallway with tables and chairs set up near the lockers," Strandlund said.

Maintaining good public relations is important once the mini-school is under way. Minneapolis officials, aware that adverse community reaction could hamper future funding, operate the mini-school as a "closed campus," forbidding girls to leave the building on lunch hours.

And school officials should advise pregnant students that the mini-school will provide them with required courses, but won't be able to afford to offer science laboratories and advanced foreign language available in regular schools. Instead, the mini-school can offer practical courses designed to meet the needs of pregnant students.

For most girls in the PACE program, the tradeoff is fine. "I'm going to be out on my own from now on," said Charlotte Miller, a senior. "I'm learning about checking accounts and where there is reduced day care. That's important because I'll be a single parent. It's better than a regular school." If PACE had not been available and Miller faced attending her regular high school, "I would have felt embarrassed," she said. "I probably would have dropped out."

This case study was researched and written by Pat Doyle, an education writer for the Minneapolis Star and Tribune.

Case Study #3

ADOLESCENT PARENTING PROGRAM

Program: The Adolescent Parenting Program, Cambridge Rindge and Latin School, Cambridge, Mass.

Summary: The program offers teen mothers an extensive parenting curriculum, an in-school day care center and a three-person social service team.

Contacts: 1. Sherry Trella or Betsy Bard, Adolescent Parenting Program, Cambridge Rindge and Latin School, 459 Broadway, Cambridge, Mass. 02138, (617)547-9200
2. Albert Giroux, director of public information, 159 Thorndike St., Cambridge, Mass. 02141, (617)498-9237

When you ask people about the Adolescent Parenting Program (APP) at Cambridge Rindge and Latin School, you hear a lot of backhanded compliments.

School Superintendent Robert S. Peterkin is "completely committed to the Adolescent Parenting Program," said his spokesman, Albert Giroux. But what Peterkin would really like to see in the 2,600-student high school, said Giroux, is a health clinic to prevent teenage pregnancy.

APP clinical social worker Betsy Bard asserted, "We're a mop-up operation. We don't offer primary prevention. We don't prevent the first pregnancy."

When the Cambridge, Mass., school board approved APP eight years ago, a minority would have preferred a pregnancy prevention program. "We couldn't find enough community support for a prevention program," recalled former school board member Alice Wolf.

But being second choice does not mean being second rate. The program offers students an extensive parenting curriculum, an in-school day care center and a three-person social service team, all helping teen mothers prepare for the future. In the 1986-87 school year, some 20 students enrolled in APP full time and an equal number used some of its services part time.

When the school district started the program seven years ago, administrators set the goals of helping teenage mothers care for their babies, graduate from high school, prevent a second pregnancy and make constructive decisions for the future.

For the most part, the program has met those goals.

In recent years, at least three-quarters of the APP students have graduated from high school. Furthermore, only a handful have gone on to a repeat pregnancy within a year and a half, far less than the national rate of 75 percent repeat pregnancies for teens. And some of the girls, once over the hump of learning to care for a newborn baby, choose to go on to college.

The program started modestly seven years ago with a home economics teacher and an instructional aide teaching child development and life coping skills.

> *"We're a mop-up operation. We don't offer primary prevention. We don't prevent the first pregnancy."*
> — Betsy Bard, APP clinical social worker

By the end of the first year, school administrators were disappointed at the program's low enrollment; fewer than 10 girls participated. School staff learned that other girls were interested but had a practical problem: they couldn't find anyone to care for their babies.

In an advocacy and fundraising effort that is a hallmark of Cambridge Rindge and Latin's program, the APP staff pushed for money from the Cambridge School Department to set up an in-school infant and toddler day care center, a center that served 16 children in the 1986-87 school year. Predictably, more girls enroll in the APP now that they can leave their children in a reliable, affordable and friendly day care center.

"If it weren't for the day care, I wouldn't have been able to come back to school," said one 18-year-old mother, a senior who is estranged from her own mother and lives on welfare benefits. During her free periods and at lunch time, she drops in at the bright, well-equipped day care center to feed and play with her baby.

While the day care center and its staff help the teen mothers stay in school, the curriculum has changed the young mothers' expectations about the future.

Though they go home from school wheeling baby carriages every day, APP students move from class to class through the high school's long hallways just like other students. But their education is not just like other students'. Half their courses the first year they're enrolled in APP are geared to teen parents although no boys have yet participated.

Adolescent Parenting Program

For example, instead of the usual social studies class, APP students take a course that teaches them about community services. APP students earn home economics credits for child development classes, health and science credits for their APP life skills class and physical education credits for a prenatal and postpartum aerobics class. In the second year in APP, the teen mothers may elect just one course designed for them: a career information course.

"APP helped me a lot," said the mother of a one-year-old boy, who admitted that she hadn't done well in school before her son was born. "I'm going to go to college. Before the baby was born, I didn't really care about school. But people here — kids and staff — really care and that makes you care."

The clinical social worker, the community liaison, the other girls and the day care staff all offer encouragement — smiles, hugs or pats on the back — whether for caring for a child with an ear infection, going through the rigorous process of signing up for welfare benefits, running for class office, or applying to college. And the girls, many of whom Bard says have poor self-esteem or poor decision-making skills, need all the encouragement they can get to stay in school and care for their babies.

> Some parents say the program encourages girls to become pregnant. "We've had one parent complain that her daughter thinks the best dressed girls in the school are the ones wearing the maternity clothes!"
> — Betsy Bard, APP clinical social worker

With the day care, the specialized courses and all its services, APP's budgets for the last two years have hovered at around $200,000 annually. That includes the expense of operating the day care center staffed at the state-mandated level of one adult for every three infants. Fortunately, the Department of Public Welfare contributes substantially to the cost of running the center through vouchers issued to eligible APP mothers.

Another state agency, the Massachusetts Department of Social Services, also contributes significantly to the overall budget by funding the social services team: the clinician, community liaison and a clerk-typist. Consequently, the school department pays a decreasing share of the program's cost — only 39 percent in fiscal year 1985-86, down from 58 percent the previous year. Minor funding comes from such sources as the federal government's occupational education program.

Despite support from its funding sources, APP has its share of critics. Some parents say the program encourages girls to become pregnant. "We've had one parent complain that her daughter thinks the best dressed girls in the school are the ones wearing the maternity clothes!" said Bard. To answer the criticism that APP makes teen pregnancy an attractive option, Bard said she interviews all the girls as they enter the program, and few are aware that APP exists when they decide to have a baby. One young mother commented, "If you're going to have a baby you're going to do it because you want to, not because the program is here."

Other implied criticism comes from school department personnel who scrutinize the Adolescent Parenting Program's budget. Sherry Trella, who administers the program, has spent weeks researching other teen parenting programs to find out if Cambridge costs are comparable. "I found that other teen parenting programs are just not as comprehensive as ours," said Trella, because they don't offer the same combination of day care, social services and an on-site parenting curriculum that lets students interact with other high school students.

"If you're going to have a baby you're going to do it because you want to, not because the program is here."

— *Teen mother*

Sherry Trella had some advice for administrators who decide to set up an adolescent parenting program. She urged starting small, using school system staff to offer courses. "In the Cambridge school system, it is existing teachers, some 20 percent of the time, some 40 percent of the time, who teach the APP program," she said.

But above all, advised Trella, anyone who wants to set up an adolescent parenting program is in for a lot of work and struggle. "You've got to be prepared to give a lot of yourself," she said one day as she grappled with the guidelines of yet another grant proposal.

This case study was researched and written by Henrietta Davis, a freelance writer based in Cambridge, Mass., who frequently writes about education.

Case Study #4

JUNIOR HIGH DECISION-MAKING CURRICULUM

Program: Decisionmaking curriculum, San Marcos, Calif., Junior High School

Summary: A four-pronged curriculum for seventh and eighth graders that is intended to help them develop the self-confidence needed to abstain from sex. The key facet of the program is a group of 180 mini-lessons for success, each 10 minutes long, that are designed to be completed daily but can be used three times a week.

Contacts: 1. B. David Brooks and Robert C. Paull, researchers, Thomas Jefferson Research Center, 1143 N. Lake Ave., Pasadena, Calif. 91104, (818)798-0791
2. Joe DeDiminicantanio, principal, and Jerry Harrington and Quality Quinn-Sharp, teachers, San Marcos Junior High School, 650 W. Mission Road, San Marcos, Calif. 92069, (619)744-1373

San Marcos, Calif., seems like the kind of place to raise a family and survive your children's teenage years.

Nestled in the rolling hills of northern San Diego County, it sports avocado groves and dairies, high-tech industries and ma-and-pa manufacturing plants. Old farm houses and cookie-cutter suburban homes nestle up to manicured parks and a pleasant retirement community complete with artificial lake, ducks and paddle boats. The biggest controversy in town is whether trash should be burned instead of buried in a landfill.

It isn't the kind of place where you'd expect to read a headline that one in every five high school girls is pregnant.

But that was the news in March 1985, sending shock waves through school administration offices and across family dinner tables, whispers in the classroom and hand-thumping in churches.

Source of the statistics was a counselor at San Marcos High School, who informally, and quite on her own, kept tally of the number of girls who had confided in her during the 1983-84 school year that they were pregnant. By year's end, the scratch marks counted 178, or about 20 percent of the female student body — double the national figures as suggested by the Alan Guttmacher

Institute and other major family planning organizations.

A disproportionate number of the pregnant girls were freshmen, leading to speculation that the pregnancy rate might have been higher because older girls who were pregnant did not confide in the counselor. Only nine of the campus pregnancies ended in childbirth; the others miscarried or were aborted, according to school officials.

William Streshly, the district superintendent at the time, gambled that it was better to share the unsettling news publicly, so the community could acknowledge and confront the problem of sexually active children, than to keep it under wraps or even ignore it.

And while there was an immediate and predictable wash of negative publicity—subjecting the San Marcos girls to ridicule from other schools that either denied or didn't know the extent of their own problem—good seems to have come from bad.

The district is betting that the most effective way to reduce the number of teenage pregnancies is for the students to say "no" to premarital sex in the first place.

Without debating the accuracy of the 20 percent pregnancy figure, San Marcos school officials say today they are well on their way in preparing their youngsters to cope with their sexuality.

The district dismissed out of hand any notion of opening on-campus health clinics that could prescribe birth control pills or make contraceptives available. It was clear that such a clinic would not be supported politically in San Marcos, nor would it reflect the perceived values of family life there. Instead, the district reinforced its high school curriculum on decisionmaking skills, hoping this step would help students deal with the question of their own sexuality.

And, deciding that the question of sexuality should be addressed on the junior high/middle school level before the battle was lost in high school, the district adopted a four-pronged curriculum for seventh and eighth graders that includes:

1. a six-week course for seventh graders on how to develop study skills, based on a program developed by the Fullerton-based Study Skills Institute of California;

2. a six-week course for eighth graders on "Sexuality, Commitment and Family," provided by Teen-Aide Inc. of Seattle, which campaigns that abstinence is the best form of birth control;

3. a six-week class for seventh graders on self esteem and values development, written by the husband-and-wife research team of Barbara Peters and Don Sharp of San Marcos; and

4. a fourth element that may well be the cement that binds the

Junior High Decisionmaking Curriculum 63

other three together. The program, intended for every classroom in the school, is "How to be Successful in Less Than Ten Minutes a Day," by B. David Brooks and Robert C. Paull of the Thomas Jefferson Research Center in Pasadena, Calif.

The district is betting that the most effective way to reduce the number of teen pregnancies (or the number of students using drugs or alcohol, for that matter) is for the students to say "no" to premarital sex (or drugs or alcohol) in the first place. The schools' role is to give students the confidence to say no by helping them to feel good about who they are, to consider the consequences of their actions and to learn how — and to have the desire to be successful in all facets of life. And that includes staying clear of the social, economic and emotional pitfalls that accompany teenage pregnancy.

Enter the Thomas Jefferson program.

The program is a collection of 180 "mini-lessons" of 10 minutes each. The authors suggest that the lessons be completed daily, perhaps in homeroom; teachers in San Marcos, who in 1986-87 are in their second year of the How to be Successful program, say it lends itself better to three times a week so the students don't burn out on it and come to resent it.

"It's not always easy to measure the benefits of the program because we're talking in terms of values, not necessarily test scores."
—*Joe DeDiminicantanio, principal, San Marcos Junior High School*

Through carefully plotted redundancy, the program calls for students to learn the STAR system of decisionmaking: Stop, Think, Act and Review. And it drums home its "12 steps to success": to be confident, responsible, present, timely, friendly, polite, prepared, a listener, a doer, a tough worker, a risk taker and a goal setter.

Throughout the series of lessons, students are prompted to prepare daily to-do lists, starting off with such items as daily homework, home chores, remembering to bring certain projects or school material to class the next day, and the like. The list concludes with such optional activities as writing to their grandmother "because that always pays off at Christmas time," as English teacher Quality Quinn-Sharp likes to quip.

The idea is for students to make attainable goals for themselves and to realize the satisfaction of reaching them, no matter how mundane. As students come to demand more of themselves, they make their to-do lists more demanding.

There is some risk that the logic might backfire; if students are unable to check off any items on their daily to-do lists, they might come to feel worse, not better, about themselves and see themselves as unsuccessful rather than successful.

"This program is not a panacea," says Joe DeDiminicantanio, principal of San Marcos Junior High School. "And it's not always easy to measure the benefits of the program because we're talking in terms of values, not necessarily test scores."

But there are some measurements, ranging from the trivial to the substantive. Quinn-Sharp is handing out fewer pencils in class; students are remembering to bring their own to school. About 90 percent of the homework assignments are being completed, compared to a 75 percent rate before the mini-lessons were introduced. And, perhaps more a reflection on the six-week study skills course that was offered last year to seventh graders, four times as many seventh graders as eighth graders were listed on the school's honor roll last spring.

Another result of the "success" program: Quinn-Sharp is grouping her students into circles of four to work together on classroom projects and problems. "The students are learning to be more cooperative with one another in exchanging ideas and helping one another," she said. "Different members of the group take on different responsibilities for the sake of the entire group" because they see how they can contribute to a successful mission.

> *Students are "learning how to live what we're teaching them in the 'success' program—that they've got to be courteous to one another, prepared, take risks, share their thoughts, to listen to one another and to desire to be the best in the class."*
>
> *— Quality Quinn-Sharp, English teacher, San Marcos Junior High School*

"They're learning how to live what we're teaching them in the 'success' program—that they've got to be courteous to one another, prepared, take risks, share their thoughts, to listen to one another and to desire to be the best in the class. Through that, we're developing skills that will help them when they grow up and find themselves in corporate board rooms," she said.

Life sciences teacher Jerry Harrington, another fan of the program, said he can see how the 'success' concepts sink in with the students. "We as parents and educators tell our kids to go out, get a good education and a good job and be successful. But we haven't done much in teaching them HOW to be successful, and that's what we're finally doing now. The kids start realizing 'Yeah, I've got to be on time, to be present, to be polite, to be friendly . . .' It starts to click with them."

Interviews with the junior high school students back this up. "It makes me consider whether I really want to quit high school to mother a child," said Shannon Riccio. Agreed Julie Delaway: "It helps you sort out your mind, your emotions and how responsibility and pregnancy have a lot to do with each other."

"You might get a reputation as a wimp if you don't" have sex, said student Kelli Duren, but as a result of the lessons, "now I'd be willing to take that risk, because it's worth it." And, according to student David Clark, "You need to risk the possibility of losing a friend, if you are asked to try something that is against your moral code."

Both Harrington and Quinn-Sharp say the program places demands on the teacher as well. "I've had to let my guard down in front of the students when I look to my own life for examples of being successful — or not being successful," Harrington said. Teachers who are less willing to share from their own life experiences might not endorse the program so heartily.

In witnessing the mini-lessons being taught, it seems that the students buy into them in direct correlation to the level of the teacher's acceptance of them. In Quinn-Sharp's class, for instance, there was no lack of waving hands to questions such

> *"I've had to let my guard down in front of the students when I look to my own life for examples of being successful — or not being successful."*
> *— Jerry Harrington, life sciences teacher, San Marcos Junior High School*

as, "Why do people want success for themselves?" ("To have a feeling of worth," said one student; "To be able to provide for yourself and your family," said another) and "How does it feel to be successful?" ("Good about who you are and what you've done," was one student's quick response).

A review of written evaluations of the program by more than 60 students suggested they were open to the course outline and usually recognized its benefit although they were critical of redundancy and the inability of some teachers to be able to take an abstract concept and make it real.

"The program makes us feel better about ourselves," said one male student, "and when we do, we don't have the incentive to go out and try to make friends in any way possible, even if that means doing drugs or having sex."

Said another, "The program didn't really teach me anything. All it taught me was to be on time and be prepared." Which is not bad, according to Principal DeDiminicantanio: "From my experience, the number one reason people lose jobs and don't hold on to their positions is because they're not on time and prepared. If I could have every kid leave school with nothing more than that, we've still done a heck of a job." He was not worried about the negative criticism, saying it simply "reflects the immaturity of the students."

Some students obviously were confused, however, by the program's challenges to "be a doer," and to "be a risk taker." More than one student wrote that they interpreted those exhortations to mean they should "do" sex and drugs because it was the "risky" thing to do.

> *"The untapped resource in our schools is our kids. Teaching them personal responsibility will help us tap that resource. We expect teachers and administrators to accomplish certain tasks, and now we're showing the kids there are tasks they have to do."*
> —*Robert C. Paull, co-author, "How to be Successful in Less Than Ten Minutes a Day"*

Co-author Robert Paull said the two-year-old program is being used in 1,600 classrooms in California and Arizona, including those in the California cities of Sacramento, Riverside, San Bernardino, Pasadena and Poway, and the Arizona communities of Scottsdale, Mesa, Tucson and Phoenix. In February 1987, it is to debut in the middle schools in St. Louis, Mo.

The program's strength, Paull said, is its use of concepts of success that can be applied in any number of situations, whether it be schoolwork, sex, drugs, alcohol, employment or even family relationships.

"The untapped resource in our schools is our kids. Teaching them personal responsibility will help us tap that resource. We expect teachers and administrators to accomplish certain tasks, and now we're showing the kids there are tasks they have to do," he said.

Other curricula address the issue of responsibility and decision-making; this one is said to be unique because of its daily, 10-minute format, according to the Thomas Jefferson researchers.

Other advantages? Hardly a day passes in San Marcos without a "success" mentality being discussed, if not in the mini-lesson itself, then in another class. The program has washed over the entire school and manifests itself daily in attitudes, behaviors and actions, according to the principal and teachers.

Junior High Decisionmaking Curriculum

The high school counselor stopped keeping track of pregnancies two years ago, so no one can say to what degree the mini-lessons on success—or any other program in the district—may be having an effect on pregnancies. But there is a clear sense in San Marcos that the crop of junior high students using the new curricula will be better prepared to face the challenges of high school.

This case study was researched and written by Tom Gorman, a San Diego-based reporter for the Los Angeles Times who has written extensively on teen pregnancy issues.

Case Study #5

TEEN THEATER TROUPE

Program: Teen Theater Troupe, New Orleans Center for Creative Arts and Planned Parenthood of Louisiana

Summary: Using the performing arts, the program tries to help high school students make responsible decisions about sexuality and other issues such as drug use, peer pressure and suicide.

Contacts: 1. Terri Bartlett, executive director, Planned Parenthood of Louisiana, Inc., 4018 Magazine St., New Orleans, La. 70115, (504)891-8013
2. Bob Cronin, teacher, or John Otis, principal, New Orleans Center for Creative Arts, 6048 Perrier St., New Orleans, La. 70118, (504)899-0055

What is it like to have a baby while you're still in high school? Drama students at the New Orleans Center for Creative Arts (NOCCA) explored that question in preparation for writing their roles in a play designed to help students make responsible decisions about sexuality.

Bob Cronin, a NOCCA theater teacher, handed each student in his second-year drama class an egg. For one week, he told them, they were to treat those eggs as if they were babies. Students would have to find appropriate care for the eggs while they were in school, at sports events or out on dates — never leaving them alone and making sure they didn't break.

By the end of the week, only about half the eggs remained unbroken, but all the students agreed they had started thinking about the responsibility involved in being a parent.

"I just laid it down on the bleachers for a minute and it rolled off," lamented one young man.

"It took up a lot of time, even as an inanimate object," said another student who returned with egg intact. "I tried to imagine what it would have been like if it was a real baby, if I'd had to feed it and dress it. I wouldn't have had time to study or see my friends or anything else."

This exercise in imagination was one part of the students' background work for a play called "Ask A Simple Question," a series of vignettes written by NOCCA students and presented to schools and community groups throughout greater New Orleans. NOCCA, a public high school, is the New Orleans version of the performing arts school featured in the movie and television series "Fame." Students from high schools around the city audition to enter NOCCA's programs in theater, dance, music, visual arts and creative writing. Those who make it into the rigorous professional program attend their "sending" schools half a day for regular academic subjects and NOCCA the other half for one of the specialized arts curricula.

Caring for an egg "took up a lot of time, even as an inanimate object. I tried to imagine what it would have been like if it was a real baby, if I'd had to feed it and dress it. I wouldn't have had time to study or see my friends or anything else."
— NOCCA student

"Ask A Simple Question" is a collaborative effort of NOCCA and the Louisiana chapter of Planned Parenthood, whose executive director, Terri Bartlett, proposed the teen theater idea to NOCCA students and staff in 1985.

As a first step, Bartlett, Cronin and two NOCCA drama students developed four scenes addressing teenage pregnancy. The students presented the scenes at an Orleans Parish School Board teenage pregnancy conference. With school board approval, the coordinators then asked second-year NOCCA students to vote on whether they wanted to adopt the project for their performance requirement.

Students approved the idea overwhelmingly and began in the fall of 1986 to devote their Wednesday afternoon theater classes to creating realistic scenes to present to their peers around the city. In addition to preparing scenes, the students heard speakers with a variety of viewpoints — those for or against legal abortion, a rape crisis counselor, a psychiatric social worker — and also went through a series of values clarification exercises with Bartlett and Cronin.

Although the teen theater troupe tackles some controversial topics, it's not expected that all students will agree on any issue, Bartlett emphasized. In fact, the students have decided not to present scenes on abortion because of a strong divergence of views within the group. And Bartlett and Cronin decided to cut some of the more sensitive scenes when the troupe performed before a junior high school audience. But on the whole, the NOCCA students are given free reign with topics and presentation. Besides teen pregnancy and sexuality, which have been the actors' main focus, the troupe also has presented scenes addressing drug use and suicide.

"The students represent the cultural and ethnic mix of our community," said Bartlett. "They know what will go and what won't go up there on stage; they have an ear for what's too corny, what comes off as racist. What they have created here is a powerful tool for communication."

At a typical performance, NOCCA students dress in jeans and T-shirts imprinted with the names of their stage characters. They act out 10 to 15 vignettes, depending on the time allotted. Topics range from date rape and peer pressure to "how to say no and mean it" and "how to talk to parents about contraceptives."

In one scene, for example, a mother sits near an imaginary wall, talking on the telephone to a friend. She used to be able to talk to her daughter about anything, she tells the friend, but now that the daughter is dating one boy, "I'm afraid she'll think I'm nosy if I ask her how involved they are."

> On the whole, the NOCCA students are given free reign with topics and presentation.

Meanwhile, the daughter sits on the other side of the imaginary wall, talking on the telephone to one of her own friends. "John and I are getting really serious," she confides. "I'm afraid something's going to happen. But I'm afraid if I ask Mom about birth control, she'll think I'm loose."

The scene ends with both mother and daughter — not hearing each other — saying in unison to their friends on the telephone, "I just wish we could talk."

Like most of the scenes the NOCCA students present, this one is left unresolved. The audience doesn't find out if mother and daughter decide to talk; in the date rape scene, the actors freeze just as the girl tells the boy to go home; in another scene, a boy worried that his girlfriend is pregnant doesn't find out for sure.

"We try to get the audience to think about the situations and come up with their own answers," said Cronin. "A lot of teenagers make their decisions by not making decisions; they let other people tell them what to do. We're not here to present any particular moralistic stance."

After all the vignettes have been presented, the actors come back on stage, remaining "in character" to answer questions from the audience.

Sometimes the questioners want to know what happened next in the vignette: "Did you tell your parents you were pregnant?" The actors try to turn the questions around and start the audience thinking: "What do you think I should have done?" At other times, the questions touch a deeper nerve: "I have a friend who was raped. Where can she go to get help?" The student actor, who has prepared for her role by visiting the YWCA's rape crisis center, tells the questioner how to get in touch with that agency. Sometimes the audience wants to know personal information about the actors themselves: "Do you use contraceptives?" At those times, one of the coordinators will step in and remind the audience that the students are actors in a play and are not there to tell their own views.

Students say coping with the emotions unleashed by the play and the question-and-answer session is the hardest part of their work. "At first I don't think any of us realized how powerful this was going to be, that we'd have people crying," said a student who is acting in the program for a second year.

"The students represent the cultural and ethnic mix of our community. They know what will go and what won't go up there on stage; they have an ear for what's too corny, what comes off as racist. What they have created here is a powerful tool for communication."

— *Terri Bartlett, executive director, Planned Parenthood of Louisiana*

"Sometimes when a parent in the audience asked me a question, I had the feeling they wished it was their own son or daughter they were asking," another student said. "It seemed they were really sincere, that they wanted to know what I thought, and that maybe asking me would give them courage to talk to their own children."

At the end of each session, the coordinators hand out evaluation sheets to the audience. The 12 questions "are designed to let those of us who put on the play know what you thought about it and to help us make it better," the sheet says.

For the teen theater troupe, "success" is defined not so much by numbers of pregnancies averted—although, because Louisiana ranks third in the nation for number of births to teenagers, that is obviously a concern—but more by whether they presented information understandably and challenged their audience to think about values. The audience circles "not at all," "somewhat" or "very much" in response to statements such as, "The characters in the play remind me of myself," and, "This play was about facts teenagers need to know to make responsible decisions about their behavior."

At the bottom of the sheet is space for the students to write a question of their own. At a Catholic high school, one girl wrote in red letters, so big that Bartlett couldn't miss it when collecting the questionnaires, "How can I tell my mother I'm pregnant?" Without revealing the student's identity, Bartlett led the assembled students in a discussion of the topic. Later Bartlett got a letter in the mail thanking her for her help.

The questionnaires led to two changes in the program for the 1986-87 school year. "When parents saw our presentation last year," Cronin said, "some of them commented that all the parent figures in our scenes came off as ogres. 'We're not like that,' they said. 'We love our kids and want to talk to them.'" After some thought, NOCCA students wrote new scenes portraying parents with more insight and sensitivity.

The other change, said Bartlett, came from realizing there was too little follow-up after the performance. Students and teachers who wanted to continue discussing the issues raised did not know where to start. To help remedy that, NOCCA and Planned Parenthood—with a $5,000 grant from the Greater New Orleans Regional Foundation—are putting together a resource handbook to be left with parents and teachers after the performances. For the students, they are printing hundreds of laminated wallet-sized cards listing the telephone numbers of area hotlines and counseling centers.

> *"We try to get the audience to think about the situations and come up with their own answers. A lot of teenagers make their decisions by not making decisions; they let other people tell them what to do. We're not here to present any particular moralistic stance."*
> —*Bob Cronin, teacher, New Orleans Center for Creative Arts*

As might be expected, "Ask A Simple Question" has generated its share of controversy in the community. Some parents, and some students, questioned the involvement of Planned Parenthood in the school, said NOCCA Principal John Otis. One church group withdrew permission for the troupe to perform in its auditorium because it believed—erroneously—that Bartlett's staff at Planned Parenthood performed abortions, Otis said. Other parents, especially those vehemently opposed to abortion, wanted the play to present more defined conclusions and not put so much emphasis on individual values.

But most of the comments Otis has heard as principal have been positive. "I have talked to parents who have told me that their children's being in the play has really opened up communication at home—not just on contraception, but in all areas," he said. For himself, Otis is pleased to see the play "take kids who are not making decisions and force them into a decisionmaking posture. The actors get the message across that students must take responsibility for themselves, to ask questions and get the information they need to make a responsible decision."

NOCCA students, as everyone who comes into contact with them is quick to point out, are a special breed. They are bright; they must maintain a B average in their sending schools to qualify to attend NOCCA. They are motivated; they work hard to get into the program, and harder still to be invited back for a second year.

And they pride themselves on their professionalism, looking with scorn upon those who merely dabble in their artistic fields. These facts acknowledged, could a program like NOCCA's teen theater troupe work in an average high school?

Students say coping with the emotions unleashed by the play and the question-and-answer session is the hardest part of their work.

NOCCA students and their adult coordinators pondered the question and came up with a qualified "yes." A teen theater program could work in a regular high school, they said, provided some extraordinary people got involved. Crucial to the program's success, they pointed out, is a skilled director. Although a teen theater project wouldn't have to be led by someone as qualified as Cronin, who has a master of fine arts degree from Smith College and has acted professionally, the task of directing the troupe might be beyond the skill of the average high school English teacher. But a dedicated, serious teacher who has some experience with play production could probably get a teen theater program off the ground, especially if the teacher were to cooperate with someone who has skills in counseling and values clarification.

Equally important, the students emphasized, was the sense of trust and respect they developed through working together. "We've really learned to listen to one another here," one said. A ground rule of the troupe from the beginning has been that "nothing gets out," that whatever they say to each other in practice sessions remains confidential. For these reasons, they thought a voluntary group — an honors English or theater class, or an after-school club — might be a more suitable setting for a teen theater project than a class students were required to attend and to which they felt little commitment.

Budget considerations, finally, need not be an obstacle. For the teen theater troupe's first year, the only cash outlay was about $100 to buy the actors' T-shirts and have their stage names printed on them. Bartlett contributed her time to the school, with her normal salary paid by Planned Parenthood. Cronin and the other drama teachers were paid their usual salaries. And NOCCA provided a van for transporting the troupe to its performance sites.

For the second year, the program received a grant for preparing education materials, and other contributions were received to cover publicity, telephone and postage expenses, food for a cast party and so on, for a total of about $7,000. Bartlett has written other grant proposals that could provide, in the future, funds for a coordinator, a part-time secretary, office space and a referral hotline. But the finances available to a teen theater group, in the end, matter less than the dedication and seriousness the actors and directors bring to the undertaking.

This case study was researched and written by Laurie Evans, formerly a copy editor for Capitol Publications, Inc., who now works as a freelance writer and editor based in Hattiesburg, Miss.

Appendices

Appendix A

Survey Results

The Education Research Group in September 1986 mailed written surveys to 5,000 school officials across the nation, seeking information on school districts' approaches to the problem of teen pregnancy. Of the 716 who responded, 79.2 percent were from rural school districts, 15 percent were from suburban school districts, and 4.6 percent were from urban school districts.

1. How many students are enrolled in your school system? (Circle One)

Response	Number of Responses	Percent of Responses
a) Fewer than 1,000	400	55.9%
b) 1,000 to 1,999	124	17.3
c) 2,000 to 5,999	114	15.9
d) 6,000 to 9,999	32	4.5
e) 10,000 or more	33	4.5
no response	13	1.9
Total	**716**	**100%**

2. What percent of the students age 11 or older in your school system do you estimate are sexually active? (Circle One)

Response	Number of Responses	Percent of Responses
a) 3 percent or less	106	14.8%
b) 4 percent to 9 percent	69	9.6
c) 10 percent to 15 percent	121	16.9
d) 16 percent to 29 percent	211	29.5
e) 30 percent to 45 percent	142	19.8
f) 46 percent or more	26	3.6
no response	41	5.8
Total	**716**	**100%**

3. What percent of the female students age 11 or older in your school system do you estimate have become pregnant in the last three years? (Circle One)

Response	Number of Responses	Percent of Responses
a) 3 percent or less	490	68.4%
b) 4 percent to 9 percent	154	21.5
c) 10 percent to 15 percent	37	5.2
d) 16 percent to 29 percent	18	2.5
e) 30 percent to 45 percent	1	0.1
f) 46 percent or more	--	--
no response	16	2.3
Total	**716**	**100%**

4. What is the high school dropout rate in your system? (Circle One)

Response	Number of Responses	Percent of Responses
a) 3 percent or less	398	55.6%
b) 4 percent to 9 percent	173	24.2
c) 10 percent to 15 percent	55	7.7
d) 16 percent to 29 percent	31	4.3
e) 30 percent to 45 percent	14	2.0
f) 46 percent or more	2	0.3
no response	43	5.9
Total	**716**	**100%**

Survey Results

5. What is your dropout rate for pregnant/parenting students? (Circle One)

Response	Number of Responses	Percent of Responses
a) 3 percent or less	531	74.2%
b) 4 percent to 9 percent	36	5.0
c) 10 percent to 15 percent	20	2.8
d) 16 percent to 29 percent	19	2.6
e) 30 percent to 45 percent	39	5.4
f) 46 percent or more	40	5.6
no response	31	4.4
Total	**716**	**100%**

6. Where would you rank teen pregnancy and teen parents on a scale with all the problems your school system faces? (Circle One)

Response	Number of Responses	Percent of Responses
a) number 1 problem we face	7	1.0%
b) among top 5 problems	155	21.6
c) among top 10 problems	156	21.8
d) among top 15 problems	96	13.4
e) not a major problem	288	40.2
no response	14	2.0
Total	**716**	**100%**

7. Does your school district offer sexuality education courses? (Circle One)

Response	Number of Responses	Percent of Responses
a) yes	409	57.1%
b) no	294	41.1
no response	13	1.8
Total	**716**	**100%**

Questions 8-12 were answered only by those who responded yes to question 7. Percentages were calculated by the total number of possible respondents to these questions (409).

8. If you answered yes to #7, are the courses (Circle One):

Response	Number of Responses	Percent of Responses
a) required	174	42.5%
b) optional, students' choice	109	26.7
c) optional, parents' choice	126	30.8
no response	---	---
Total	**409**	**100%**

Survey Results

9. If sexuality education courses are required, at what grade does the requirement begin? (Circle One)

Response	Number of Responses	Percent of Responses
a) kindergarten to grade 4	35	8.6%
b) grade 5	43	10.5
c) grade 6	23	5.6
d) grade 7	59	14.4
e) grade 8	21	5.1
f) grade 9	37	9.0
g) grades 10 to 12	36	8.8
h) not applicable	105	25.7
no response	50	12.3
Total	**409**	**100%**

10. If sexuality education courses are optional, at what grade do they begin? (Circle One)

Response	Number of Responses	Percent of Responses
a) kindergarten to grade 4	28	6.8%
b) grade 5	59	14.4
c) grade 6	20	4.9
d) grade 7	42	10.3
e) grade 8	14	3.4
f) grade 9	45	11.0
g) grades 10 to 12	46	11.2
h) not applicable	90	22.0
no response	65	16.0
Total	**409**	**100%**

11. In what department are your sexuality education courses offered? (Circle One)

Response	Number of Responses	Percent of Responses
a) health	297	72.6%
b) physical education	15	3.7
c) science	33	8.1
d) other*	207	28.9

Many respondents indicated their school districts offer sexuality education courses in more than one department. To avoid counting a school system twice, percentages for responses (a), (b) and (c) were calculated based on 409 respondents, and the percentage for response (d) was calculated separately, based on the total number of survey respondents (716).

12. Do you think the sexuality education available in your school district reduces teen pregnancy? (Circle One)

Response	Number of Responses	Percent of Responses
a) yes, but it's just a hunch	272	66.5%
b) yes, and I have substantial evidence to support my belief	24	5.9
c) no, but it's just a hunch	107	26.2
d) no, and I have substantial evidence to support my belief	10	2.4
e) no, in fact sex education encourages teen pregnancy	7	1.7
Total*	**420**	**102.7%**

Eleven respondents who answered no to question 7 decided to respond to this question even though their school districts do not offer sexuality education courses. Percentages were calculated based on 409 eligible respondents so that they would be comparable to the other questions about sexuality education courses.

Note: Because respondents were asked to circle as many responses for questions 13-15 as apply to their situation, percentages do not equal 100. All percentages for questions 13-15 are based on the total number of respondents (716).

13. Which of the following services do you think are most effective for pregnant teens and teen parents? (Circle as many as apply)

Response	Number of Responses	Percent of Responses
a) alternative schools	158	22.1%
b) personal counseling	514	71.8
c) intensive parenting education and family planning	427	59.6
d) referrals	231	32.3
e) child care	168	23.5
f) other	53	7.4

14. Which services does your district provide? (Circle as many as apply)

Response	Number of Responses	Percent of Responses
a) alternative schools	159	22.2%
b) personal counseling	560	78.2
c) intensive parenting education and family planning	140	19.6
d) referrals	384	53.6
e) child care	76	10.6
f) other	92	12.8

15. Which services do you think you'd receive the most community/parental opposition to? (Circle as many as apply)

Response	Number of Responses	Percent of Responses
a) alternative schools	256	35.8%
b) personal counseling	50	7.0
c) intensive parenting education and family planning	347	48.5
d) referrals	48	6.7
e) child care	212	29.9
f) other	74	10.3

16. Do you believe pregnant teens and teen parents should be educated in the mainstream, alongside other students? (Circle One)

Response	Number of Responses	Percent of Responses
a) yes	574	80.2%
b) yes, but exclude them from extracurricular activities	56	7.8
c) separate for the most part, but allow some interaction	58	8.1
d) no, in all cases	18	2.5
no response	9	1.4
Total	**716**	**100%**

17. What do you believe to be the effect of mainstreaming pregnant teens and teen parents? (Circle One)

Response	Number of Responses	Percent of Responses
a) encourages other teens to get pregnant	63	8.8%
b) discourages other teens from getting pregnant	181	25.3
c) no effect either way	444	62.0
no response	28	3.9
Total	**716**	**100%**

18. Should birth control be provided to students as part of comprehensive health clinic services? (Circle One)

Response	Number of Responses	Percent of Responses
a) yes	195	27.2%
b) no	282	39.4
c) yes, but only with parents' permission	218	30.4
no response	21	3.0
Total	**716**	**100%**

19. Does your school district provide birth control to students as part of comprehensive health clinic services? (Circle One)

Response	Number of Responses	Percent of Responses
a) yes	8	1.1%
b) no	689	96.2
c) yes, but only with parents' permission	10	1.4
no response	9	1.3
Total	**716**	**100%**

Appendix B

Bibliography

"The Adolescent Family Life Demonstration Projects: Program and Evaluation Summaries," Washington, D.C.: Office of Population Affairs, 1986.

Bennett, David A., and Wanda Miller. "School Clinics Help Curb Teen Pregnancy and Dropout Rates." The School Administrator, Vol. 43, No. 8, p. 12, Arlington, Va.: American Association of School Administrators, September 1986.

Boethius, Carl Gustaf. "Sex Education in Swedish Schools: The Fact and the Fiction." Family Planning Perspectives, Vol. 17, No. 6, p. 276, New York City: Alan Guttmacher Institute, November/December 1985.

Dawson, Deborah Ann. "The Effects of Sex Education on Adolescent Behavior." Family Planning Perspectives, Vol. 18, No. 4, p. 162, New York City: Alan Guttmacher Institute, July/August 1986.

Demsko, Tobin W. "School-Based Health Clinics: A Look at the Johns Hopkins Study" (preliminary draft), Washington, D.C.: Family Research Council, 1986.

Dryfoos, Joy. "School-Based Health Clinics: A New Approach to Preventing Adolescent Pregnancy." Family Planning Perspectives, Vol. 17, No. 2, p. 70, New York City: Alan Guttmacher Institute, March/April 1985.

Dryfoos, Joy. "School Systems Take on Pregnancy Prevention." The School Administrator, Vol. 43, No. 8, p. 24, New York City: Alan Guttmacher Institute, September 1986.

"Fort Worth Independent School District Adolescent Pregnancy Advisory Committee Report to the Board of Education," Ft. Worth, Texas: Fort Worth Independent School District, 1983.

Hadley, Elaine, et. al. "School-Based Health Clinics: A Guide to Implementing Programs," Washington, D.C.: Center for Population Options, 1986.

Hayes, Cheryl D. Risking the Future: Adolescent Sexuality, Pregnancy, and Childbearing. Washington, D.C.: National Academy of Sciences, 1986.

Jones, Elise, et. al. "Teenage Pregnancy in Developed Countries: Determinants and Policy Implications." Family Planning Perspectives, Vol. 17, No. 2, p. 53, New York City: Alan Guttmacher Institute, March/April 1985.

Kenney, Asta M., and Margaret Terry Orr. "Sex Education: An Overview of Current Programs, Policies and Research." Phi Delta Kappan, Vol. 65, No. 7, p. 491, Bloomington, Ind.: Phi Delta Kappa, March 1984.

"Life Planning Education: A Strategy for Teenage Pregnancy Prevention." Washington, D.C.: Center for Population Options, 1986.

Makinson, Carolyn. "The Health Consequences of Teenage Fertility." Family Planning Perspectives, Vol. 17, No. 3, p. 132, New York City: Alan Guttmacher Institute, May/June 1985.

Marsiglio, William, and Frank L. Mott. "The Impact of Sex Education on Sexual Activity, Contraceptive Use and Premarital Pregnancy Among American Teenagers." Family Planning Perspectives, Vol. 18, No. 4, p. 151, New York City: Alan Guttmacher Institute, July/August 1986.

Mosbacker, Barrett. "Teen Pregnancy and School-Based Health Clinics." Washington, D.C.: Family Research Council, 1986.

Mott, Frank L., and William Marsiglio. "Early Childbearing and Completion of High School." Family Planning Pespectives, Vol. 17, No. 5, p. 234, New York City: Alan Guttmacher Institute, September/October 1985.

Muraskin, Laura. "Sex Education Mandates: Are They the Answer?" Family Planning Perspectives, Vol. 18, No. 4, p. 171, New York City: Alan Guttmacher Institute, July/August 1986.

"1985-86 Report to the Community," Albuquerque, N.M.: New Futures High School, 1986.

"Parental Involvement." Clinic News, Vol. 2, No. 3, p. 3, Washington, D.C.: Support Center for School-Based Clinics, October 1986.

Polit, Denise F., and Janet R. Kahn. "Project Redirection: Evaluation of a Comprehensive Program for Disadvantaged Teenage Mothers." Family Planning Perspectives, Vol. 17, No. 4, p. 150, New York City: Alan Guttmacher Institute, July/August 1985.

"Public Concerns About Family Planning Programs and Teens." Issues in Brief, Vol. 5, No. 4, p. 1, Washington, D.C.: Alan Guttmacher Institute, January 1985.

Rossitt, Jeannie I., and Asta M. Kenney. "Title X and Its Critics." Family Planning Perspectives, Vol. 16, No. 3, p. 111, New York City: Alan Guttmacher Institute, May/June 1984.

"School Based Clinic Policy Initiatives Around the Country: 1985." Washington, D.C.: Center for Population Options, January 1986.

"School-Based Clinics: Update." Washington, D.C.: Support Center for School-Based Clinics, 1986.

Sonenstein, Freya L., and Karen J. Pittman. "The Availability of Sex Education in Large School Districts." Family Planning Perspectives, Vol. 17, No. 1, p. 19, New York City: Alan Guttmacher Institute, January/February 1985.

"Teenage Pregnancy: 500,000 Births a Year and Few Tested Programs," Gaithersburg, Md.: U.S. General Accounting Office, 1986.

Weatherley, Richard, et. al. "Comprehensive Programs for Pregnant Teenagers and Teenage Parents: How Successful Have They Been?" Family Planning Perspectives, Vol. 18, No. 2, p. 73, New York City: Alan Guttmacher Institute, March/April 1986.

"What Government Can Do About Teenage Pregnancy." Issues In Brief, Vol. 4, No. 2, p. 1, Washington, D.C.: Alan Guttmacher Institute, March 1984.

Wilson, Susan. "Creating Family Life Education Programs in the Public Schools: A Guide for State Education Policy Makers." Alexandria, Va.: National Association of State Boards of Education, 1985.

Zabin, Laurie S., et. al. "Evaluation of a Pregnancy Prevention Program for Urban Teenagers." Family Planning Perspectives, Vol. 18, No. 3, p. 119, New York City: Alan Guttmacher Institute, May/June 1986.

Appendix C

From Our Rolodex

The following organizations can provide reams of statistical information and other data for school districts interested in starting or revising their teen pregnancy or parenting programs.

Alan Guttmacher Institute
2010 Massachusetts Ave. NW
Suite 500
Washington, D.C. 20036
(202)296-4012

Alan Guttmacher Institute
111 Fifth Ave.
New York, N.Y. 10003-1089
(212)254-5656

Children's Defense Fund
122 C St. NW
Suite 400
Washington, D.C. 20001
(202)628-8787

Center for Population Options
1012 14th St. NW
Suite 1200
Washington, D.C. 20005
(202)347-5700

House Select Committee on Children, Youth and Families
Rep. George Miller, D-Calif., chairman
House Office Building, Annex 2
Room 385
Washington, D.C. 20515
(202)226-7660

Planned Parenthood of America
810 7th Ave.
New York, N.Y. 10019
(212)541-7800

The IMPACT ON THE SCHOOLS series — tough issues tackled head-on —

From the Education Research Group

☐ **YES**, I need to know how my colleagues are dealing with the teenage pregnancy issue. Please rush me *Teen Pregnancy: Impact on the Schools*.

Also available:

☐ **Teen Pregnancy: Impact on the Schools** — $29.95

☐ **The Child Abuse Crisis: Impact on the Schools** — $35.00
Covers what states and districts are doing to detect and eliminate child abuse, the benefits and problems with the screening laws and the legal responsibilities of reporting child abuse cases.

☐ **P.L. 94-142: Impact on the Schools** — $55.00
Has the Education for All Handicapped Children Act accomplished what it set out to do? Who has it helped? Who has it hurt?

☐ **AIDS: Impact on the Schools** — $45.50
What are the facts behind the issue that has led some schools to act out of fear? This book explores what is safe and what isn't, what precautions to take and which ones are just plain unnecessary.

☐ **All four books (at 20% off!)** — $132.00

☐ Check enclosed (payable to Capitol Publications, Inc.)
☐ Bill me/my organization

Purchase order number _____

☐ Charge ☐ VISA ☐ MasterCard ☐ American Express

Account number _____

Signature (required for billing and credit orders) _____

Expiration date _____

Telephone _____

For fastest service, call
TOLL-FREE 1-800-327-7204
M-F, 9-5 EST. In Virginia, call collect (703) 739-6500.

Name _____
Organization _____
Address _____
City _____ State _____ ZIP _____

Education Research Group, Capitol Publications, Inc.
1101 King St., P.O. Box 1453, Alexandria, VA 22313-2053